W9-BTN-214

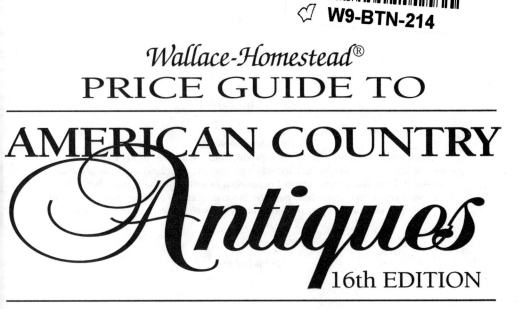

Wallace-Homestead®
PRICE GUIDE TO
AMERICAN COUNTRY
Antiques
16th EDITION

DON & CAROL RAYCRAFT

© 1999 by
Don and Carol Raycraft

All rights reserved.
No portion of this publication may be reproduced or transmitted in any form or by any
means, electronic or mechanical, including photocopy, recording, or any information
storage and retrieval system, without permission in writing from the publisher, except
by a reviewer who may quote brief passages in a critical article or review to be printed in
a magazine or newspaper, or electronically transmitted on radio or television.

Published by

krause
publications

700 E. State Street • Iola, WI 54990-0001
Telephone: 715/445-2214

Please call or write for our free catalog. Our toll-free number
to place an order or obtain a free catalog is 800-258-0929
or please use our regular business telephone 715-445-2214
for editorial comment and further information.

Library of Congress Catalog Number: 86-640023
ISBN: 0-87341-761-5
Printed in the United States of America

Cover photograph by: Carol Raycraft

CONTENTS

ACKNOWLEDGMENTS

The authors would like to sincerely thank the individuals and businesses below for their help in putting this project together. It is a complex process and could not be completed without their help.

Bruce & Vicki Waasdorp
Jim Beedy
Duane Watson
Teri & Joe Dziadul
American Roots
Tony Macek
Aston Macek Auction Co.
Early Spring Farm
Allen & Linc Hanson
Michael & Seth Fallon
Copake Auction, Inc.
Baker & Co.
Tom Baker
Judie Dilworth
Mary Lou & John Finnigan
Jim Livesey
Kathey Sarr
Simply Country Antiques Show
Carolyn Stone
Kathy Hind
Liberty Tree Antiques
Vera Gardiner & Cathy Hiller
Collectors' Choice Antique
    Gallery
Andrea Hollenbaugh
RC Raycraft
Tony A. Uphoff Jr.
Bobby & Vixen Farling

Wesley Hanback
Jim White
A. Gridley Antiques
Alex Hood
Natcho Campbell
Cyril Zoerner
Dr. Ben Gentry
Joyce Steiner
Nancy Draper
Tony & Diane Alexander
Julie Bishop
Dr. Alan Weintraub DVM
T.A. Uphoff
E.L. Raycraft
E.M. Faulkner
Opal Pickens
Michael & Emily Raycraft

Photography
Joe Dziadul
Jim Beedy
Duane Watson
Tony Macek
Bruce Waasdorp
Don Raycraft
Luke Troyer
Rusty Bartels

CHAPTER 1

*I*NTRODUCTION

Since the first edition of this book in 1978, there have been significant changes in the way most of us collect antiques and Americana.

1. Collectibles malls have proliferated like weeds in an untended garden in locations ranging from abandoned super markets to bankrupt Yugo dealerships. Many of the malls feature extensive collections of contemporary magazines, beanie animals, and discarded McDonald's Happy Meal boxes in their original sacks. Others shoot themselves in their collective feet by adding crafts to the mix. The combination of baseball cards, plywood ducks, and bundles of weeds fashioned into holiday wreaths draws a crowd that resembles any Wal-Mart in Arkansas on the Saturday night before Christmas.

2. Painted surfaces are at the top of the shopping lists of most serious Americana collectors. Refinished country pine no longer is desirable, but many of these pieces have been given new respectability along with several fresh and distressed coats of paint. In recent years, shades of white and blue have been especially popular.

In 1978, if you collected painted furniture it did not take a substantial amount of knowledge to be successful. Mainly because few dry sinks, cupboards, benches, or bowls had been repainted or had their paint remnants enhanced to increase their value. In most instances, you could assume that your purchase was what it was purported to be. Unfortunately, today that is no longer the situation. In addition to a bulbous checking account, you need some knowledge or good advice.

3. The home decorating or shelter magazines that proliferated in the 1980s have been able to influence the tastes of their readers to the point that many dealers have seen "runs" on certain examples of Americana. These areas of special interest include:

   a. Country furniture with several coats of white paint is popular. Typically it is not crucial how long ago the painted surface was applied on the piece or its overall condition. It is critical only that the piece have the "look."

   b. A variation of lodge or cabin "antiques" have been heavily promoted in the 1990s. Worn and tattered Indian blankets from Sears that date from the 1940s are combined with used furniture wrapped in pealing

5

paint. A cross-section of sporting collectibles that include bowling trophies and mounted squirrels are added as accents. The Copenhagen tobacco print advertisements of the late 1990s could serve as a textbook for this "look."

c. Garden benches, fountains, plant stands, tools, baskets, bird houses, and random pieces of fencing have been popular collectibles for individuals attempting to recapture an era that they never experienced in the first place. Most of the garden related collectibles have been made from cast iron, concrete, wood, or wire. Some were made last Tuesday and others date from the early twentieth century. If you are only collecting a "look" it doesn't make any difference. Most of the shelter magazines have the ability to put a variety of items together in a cover picture that makes it almost mandatory for the reader to attempt to duplicate it.

We know some dealers who have the similar skill to decorate their booth at antiques shows. They are on a first name basis with shabby "chic" cupboards, baskets, and firkins and can put together a room setting that is tasteful and attractive in that environment.

The problem for the collector occurs when the item is transported from the booth to the home and the buyer then attempts to integrate it into an existing collection. It quickly becomes obvious that the item does not look as good in the home as it did in the show booth. It is our belief that many of the shelter magazines are much more concerned with a "look" than authenticity. They consistently push "looks" or trends to keep you buying the magazine in much the same way that fashion editors and designers manipulate the width of ties or the length of skirts.

4. The concept of tailgating has a long history at college football games across America, but is relatively new in the world of buying and selling antiques. Initially some promoters of large antiques shows were less than enthusiastic when another entrepreneur rented a motel across the street from their "big" show and filled all of the rooms with dealers. They perceived this as competition that would detract from their gate rather than enhancing it.

Several promoters did not comprehend that their show became even more of an attraction when there were an additional 50-100 dealers next door selling comparable merchandise. The opportunity to see the wares of 150-200 dealers becomes a regional event, rather than just another "big" show. In addition, customers are willing to attend from a far wider geographic area. If more tailgates are added to the mix, the series of events can become national in scope with customers flying in from around the United States to buy from 400-500 dealers. The three current leaders among the "big" show and tailgates are Antique Week in New Hampshire, the York Antiques Show in Pennsylvania, and the Heart of Country held in Nashville in February and October.

The New Hampshire shows are held in and around Manchester in early August. The New Hampshire Dealers' Show is the primary event with five other "tailgates" opening at various points during Antique Week. Several of the tailgates could stand alone as outstanding individual Americana shows. The combination of six shows in a seven day period draws collectors nationwide.

The potential problem that faces the New Hampshire and Nashville events is that as they continue to grow in number of shows and dealers, the size of the crowd does not automatically increase at the same rate. Each year similar crowds with similar dollars to spend are spread over an extra 25-50 dealers. At some point, there will be dealers who are going to fall by the wayside because of declining sales. The merchandise at Manchester and Nashville is typically high and the customers that travel to both venues are usually semi-serious to serious buyers. The casual Sunday afternoon "tire kickers" won't find many depression glass dealers at either event.

The York Antique Show is one of the country's premier Americana events and the tailgate at a local Holiday Inn compliments it. The tailgate promoter rents the motel and then offers its rooms to dealers from throughout New England, New York and Pennsylvania with a sprinkling of other vendors from the South and Midwest. The number of dealers at the tailgate and the "big" show at the fairgrounds seem to match well with the size of the crowd each year.

Prices

The primary purpose of any price guide is to give the reader some insight and general awareness of the approximate value of a given item. The price is not exact or precise, but should be within the "ball park." Value is determined only at that point when you decide how much you want, and I decide if I am willing to pay your price. If I buy a blue dry sink at one of the shows in New Hampshire during Antique Week or a comparable example in a small shop in southern Illinois, I will not pay the same price. There can be significant geographic influences on value that must be taken into consideration in the pricing process.

The prices in this book have, for the most part, been supplied by the dealers' selling the merchandise that is illustrated. The auction prices reflect what the piece brought on a given day when it was sold. We do not know if the price was inflated by ego or emotionally driven bidding between two or three people who didn't particularly like each other that day. Several sections in this edition have been included that reflect prices provided by collectors.

Regardless of the prices' origins, use any books with prices only as a guide and not a bible. Guides have a tendency to change over time, and bibles are pretty much carved in stone with little flexibility. In the long run, it will be the "finding" and not the "buying" that is the highlight of the antique experience.

CHAPTER 2

ANTIQUES 104

Evaluating Americana

In evaluating any piece of Americana, there are four critical aspects of it that must be closely examined. It doesn't make any difference if it is a dry sink, trade sign, or mortar and pestle, the process is the same. Over time, every collector develops standards that usually are not negotiable. These differ from person to person, but it doesn't make any difference if the evaluation of the piece is taken through the same steps.

The areas of concern are authenticity, surface, color, and degree of rarity.

Authenticity

1. Is the piece what it is alleged to be by the seller?
2. Is it representative of the period in which it was supposedly made?
3. Have there been any additions, subtractions, or structural changes to it?
4. Do you have enough knowledge to appreciate what may make the piece unusual or especially desirable?

Surface

1. If the piece is unpainted, are there any traces of a painted fin-ish that were removed at some point?
2. If the piece is unpainted, can you live with its appearance and patina?
3. If the piece is painted, is the current paint original to the piece or has it been overpainted?
4. If the piece is painted, can you live with the texture of the paint?
5. Is the surface too "rough" to your taste?

Color

1. Can you live with the color of the piece?
2. Is there enough paint on the piece or does it have only remnants of its original paint?
3. If the piece is painted blue, red or yellow, are you positive that it has not been repainted, enhanced or "moved around"?

Degree of Rarity

1. Does this piece have some characteristics that make it especially unique?
2. Have you seen other similar examples so you have a standard of comparison?

3. Is the piece so rare that your standards can be relaxed to some degree?

What's Hot?

1. Stone fruit
2. Indiana hickory furniture
3. Odd Fellows' initiation regalia
4. Painted furniture
5. Krispy Kremes
6. Color, surface, condition
7. Sporting antiques & collectibles
8. Significant rarities in every collecting category
9. New Hampshire, Nashville, & York, PA antiques shows with tailgates or satellite events
10. The gradual return of quality general line antiques shops

What's Not?

1. Food at most antiques shows
2. Anything Shaker made for the "world."
3. Containers from Europe filled with broken goat carts and galvanized watering cans.
4. The rap version of "Bridge Over Troubled Water."
5. Antiques malls in abandoned auto parts stores
6. Surfaces that have been refinished or repainted

7. Refrigerator Perry
8. Shopping mall craft shows
9. Mediocre antiques & collectibles
10. Garage sales in East St. Louis, Illinois

What's Going To Be?

1. "Primitives" from around the world with a painted surface
2. Tin kitchenware
3. Pond boats
4. Felt pennants with sewn letters
5. Furniture from the first half of the 20th century until it's gone, and then furniture & accessories from the second half of the century.
6. A growing appreciation for the concept that less is probably more.

What's Not Going To Be?

1. Anything that resembles a beanie baby
2. Motivational speeches by O. J. Simpson
3. Lower-end merchandise of any kind
4. Crafts malls
5. Shows with 75 craft exhibitors, 5 chiropractors, 2 aluminum siding salesmen, and 18 beanie baby dealers

A Scholarly Guide To Collector Personality Characteristics

We have spent a significant amount of time sifting through the most recent national census data (1962) that has been made available to us. Our goal was to accurately secure some insights into a personality profile of individuals who collect specific categories of antiques and collectibles. We have made extensive use of sophisticated statistical tools (measures of central tendency) to accurately represent our target population and their characteristics. For those unfamiliar with the terminology, measures of central tendency include mean, median, and mode.

	Carnival Glass Collectors	Painted Furniture Collectors	Shaker Collectors	Beanie Babies Collectors
Favorite Singing Group	Manheim Steamroller	Beatles	3 Tenors	Wayne Newton, Alabama
Occupation	Retired Sales	Lawyer	Physician	Asst. Manager at Denny's
Automobile	Oldsmobile 88	Jeep Grand Cherokee	Range Rover	Dodge Van
Favorite Actor(s)	Tim Allen, Debbie Reynolds	Harrison Ford	Meryl Streep William Boyd	Jim Varney, John Wayne
Alma Mater	Pasadena Junior College (California)	Penn State, Northwestern	Dartmouth	South Shore High School (Chicago, IL)
Favorite Color	Orange	Blue	Grey	White
Favorite Publication	Arizona Highways, Reader's Digest	Maine Antiques Digest	N.Y. Times Town and Country	National Enquirer
Other Areas of Interest	Cats, National Geographic Magazine, Precious Moments	Activities at the "Club," Golf	Planned Parenthood ACLU, AMA	Activities at the Legion, Hallmark Ornaments, Mixed League Bowling

If you are going to collect country antiques, these are the rules.

* The four key words to memorize are "What's your best price?" The eight word version is "Is that the best that you can do?"
* Cultivate pickers or dealers to call you if they find something "special" within your category of collecting.
* Let people know that you are serious about your areas of interest.
* Eventually you will realize that the key to collecting is the finding and not the buying.
* If you are a huge fan of Precious Moments or beanie babies, don't tell anybody. Stay in the closet as long as possible.
* It is critical to get into the antiques show or market as quickly as possible before it has been completely "picked." Take advantage of any "early bird" admission that is offered.

* To keep abreast of shows, markets, and antiques-related events subscribe to the *Maine Antiques Digest*, *New Town Bee*, or the Ohio-based *Antiques Review*.
* If you finally find an item and it meets all your expectations, buy it. In today's troubled market, it is always easier to come up with the money than the stuff. If you are going to keep it "forever," you can't pay too much.
* If you have concerns about a particular piece, don't buy it. Questions tend to persist and multiply after you get it home. Some spouses also have a tendency to bring it up when tensions elevate within the friendly confines.
* Make it a point to secure a detailed and dated receipt for everything you purchase. Keep all the receipts someplace where

you can find them. At some point you (or your heirs) will need them in a hurry.

* We had a friend once who truly believed, "There is something great in every shop at a good price." He was wrong then, and is especially wrong today.
* If you are buying to replicate a shelter magazine promoted "look" for your home, you will probably sell your purchases for considerably less than you paid.
* We have always been intrigued by the opportunity to write a check with no identification 500 miles from home at a shop (or at a show for, $800) and needing three forms of identification to write a check for, $8 at the chain store two blocks from our house where we shop everyday.

Stone Fruit

In the early spring of 1998, we went to Italy with some friends on a tour of Tuscany, Florence, and Rome. We had numerous opportunities to visit shops in the villages of Tuscany and the urban area. Several Sunday flea markets and a show in the parking garage in Rome were on our itinerary. Our primary antiques focus was on adding some stone fruit to our collection. Over a period of twelve days we did not see a single piece of "old" stone fruit. Even "new" stone fruit was not in great quantity.

In the Tuscan village of Cortona, we found a shop on the cobblestone square that had a large bowl of stone fruit in the window. The lady who owned the shop had limited familiarity with English, but was able to say "Not old, not antique." It took a close examination of her fruit collection to reach the same conclusion. Absolutely the only difference between the "old" and the "new" was sixty years of exposure to sun, dust, and a periodic bump. The quality of the painted surfaces and workmanship was almost identical.

"Old" stone fruit dates from the late 1800s and early 1900s during the dwindling days of the Victorian emphasis on "more is more" when furnishing a home. The "new" stone fruit was generally, $20-$25 for each piece and we saw no half pieces, watermelon slices, oversized or miniature pieces of fruit. It has been our experience that more "old" and affordable stone fruit turns up in California at this writing than in the Midwest or on the East Coast.

Degrees of Rarity

Off the Charts Rare	Uncommon	Fairly Common
pineapples	cherries	apples
slices of watermelon	limes	bananas
	strawberries	bunches of grapes
Rare	walnuts	figs
half pieces		oranges
miniature pieces		pears
oversized pieces		

Walnuts, $30-$40 (each).

Oversized strawberry, $45-$55.

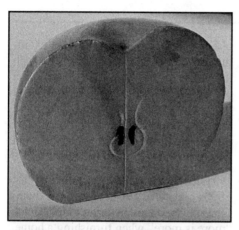

Strawberries, $30-$35 (each).

One-half apple, $375-$425.

Peach, $30-$35.

Apple, $40-$45.

Apple, $40-$45.

Banana, $35-$40.

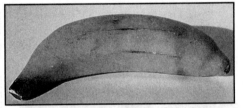

Banana, $35-$40.

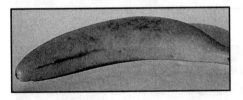

Banana, $35-$40.

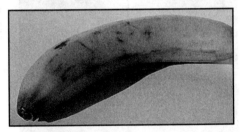

Banana, $35-$40.

Grapes, $70-$75.

Grapes, $60-$65.

Green fig, $35-$45.

Figs & walnuts, $35-$45 (figs); $30-$40 (walnuts).

Rare lemon that is made of two halves, $450-$550.

Extremely rare apple with stone leaf, $800-$900.

Odd Fellow Memorabilia

The International Order of Odd Fellows was established in the nineteenth century as a fraternal organization for men. There were hundreds of chapters throughout the United States in the years after World War I. The Odd Fellows established orphanages, schools, and long-term care centers for senior members and their wives.

Almost every rural and urban community in the Midwest had successful chapters. It is still possible in small town Illinois to drive down a street in business districts and see the I.O.O.F. signs in the second floor windows of buildings. The standard procedure was to construct a building and place the lodge hall on an upper floor with the first floor rented to a furniture store, drug emporium, or professional office. After World War II and the advent of television, hard roads, and declining small town businesses, the Odd Fellows slowly lost membership.

The decade of the 1990s saw a growing interest from Americana collectors in Odd Fellow memorabilia. Of special interest to folk art collectors are selected pieces of regalia used in the initiation of new members. These items include podiums, carvings, intricate staffs, and furniture.

Several years ago, a friend took us to his uncle's Odd Fellows lodge that was down to three members. We had an extensive tour of the bottom floor and a look at the original meeting area on the second floor. Due to lack of use, the area had fallen into disrepair. The members were pleased to show off some of the Odd Fellows' memorabilia, but became reticent when we asked for a look inside the regalia closet. The key had been mysteriously misplaced, and after a brief search, it was determined that we would have to visit the closet on our next trip upstairs.

As you might expect that event was not to be, the uncle passed away shortly after our pilgrimage to the lodge and it was closed. The contents and regalia were returned to the Grand Lodge and eventually sold by sealed bid. (We didn't win that day either.) Many of the items illustrated in this section are from the inventory and collection of Tony and Diane Alexander of Paris, Illinois. The Alexander's have been buying and selling I.O.O.F. memorabilia for more than a decade and are nationally known.

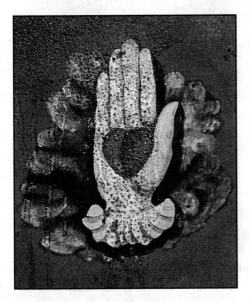

Heart in Hand on Odd Fellows podium.

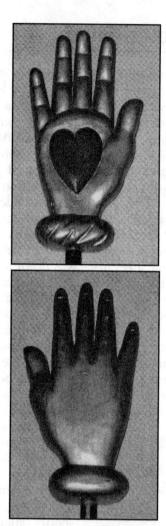

Gold hand, closed fingers, red heart, carved cuff on staff, c. early 1900s, $1,500-$2,000.

Gold hand, open fingers, red heart, gold cuff on black staff, c. early 1900s, $1,500-$2,000.

Gold hand, closed fingers, red heart, folded thumb, blue cuff on black staff, c. early 1900s, $1,500-$2,000.

Odd Fellows interlocking symbol, c. 1920s, $275-$325.

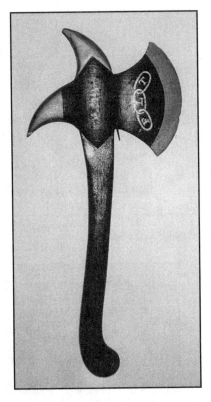

Wooden ax with painted interlocking chain, c. 1930, $300-$400.

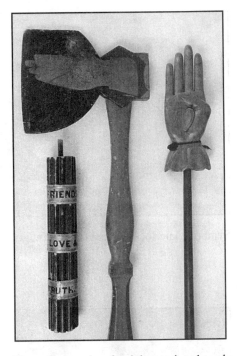

Unusual bunch of sticks, painted and damaged ax, gold hand and heart on a black staff, c. early 1900s, sticks, $150-175; ax, $300-425; heart in hand, $1,500-$2,000.

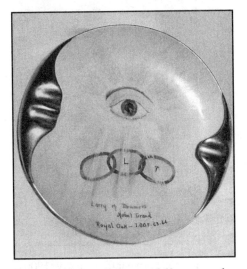

Cigar-cigarette ashtray, c. 1960, personalized, $30-$40.

Odd Fellows podium from lodge in Tennessee, c. early 1900s, $2,000-$3,000.

Symbolic interlocking chain, c. 1920s, good, painted gold, $200-$250.

Sword with hanging scales of justice, c. 1920s, wooden sword, $400-$550.

Ram's horn staff, c. early 1900s, $500-$750.

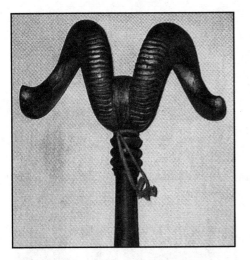

Ram's horn staff, c. early 1900s, $500-$750.

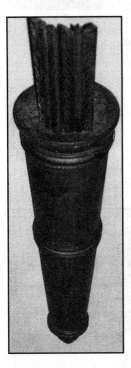

Wooden quiver and arrows, c. early 1900s, red quiver & gold arrows, $400-$500.

Set of painted Odd Fellows sticks from initiation process, c. 1920, $100-$125.

Cornucopia from Odd Fellows auxiliary, c. 1900, rare, $1,200-$1,800.

Ohio meeting hall lantern from Odd Fellows auxiliary, c. 1900, $400-$475.

Rare cast iron Odd Fellows cookie mold, c. late nineteenth century, $400-$500.

Well done Odd Fellows carved & painted ceremonial "ark," c. 1920, $500-$600 (Aston Macek Auctioneers & Appraisers).

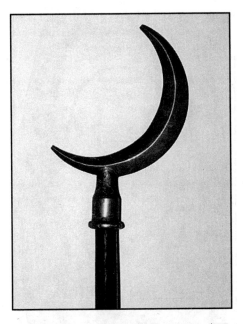

Metal "half moon" on staff, c. 1920, $75-$85.

Metal star on staff, c. 1920, $75-$85.

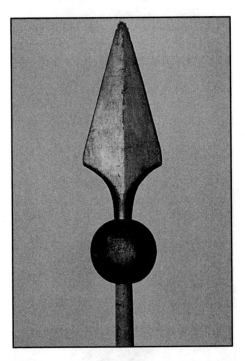

Wooden staff with turned ball painted gold, c. 1900, $50-$65.

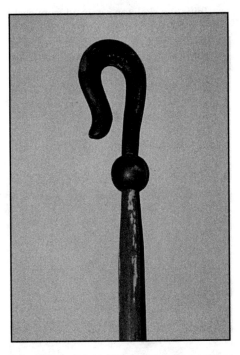

Wooden staff painted red with golden turned ball and top, c. 1900, $50-$65.

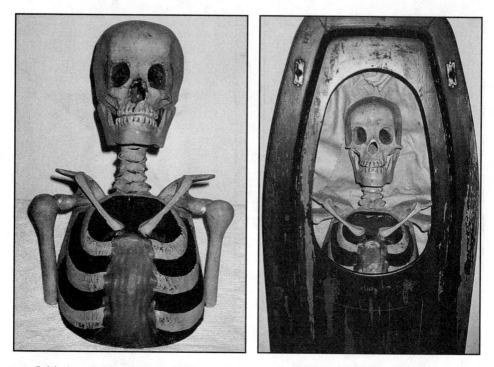

Initiation skeleton removed from casket, c. early 1900s, $300-$400 (with casket).

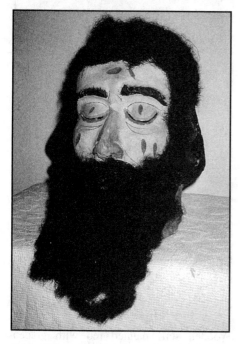

Initiation mask, c. early 1900s, $85-$100.   Initiation mask, c. early 1900s, $85-$100.

Oak chair from I.O.O.F. meeting room, c. 1915, $135-$150.

I.O.O.F. flag, used on member's grave on Memorial Day, c. 1950s, pristine condition, $15-$20.

A Picker's Baker's Dozen

At first glance the life of a "picker" appears to many of us to be almost ideal. The picker gets to go from shop to tag sale to auction to house call with the intent of finding treasures and then offering the purchases to clients for a significant profit. It is not hard to visualize the picker returning to his/her treasure filled home each night with a van or truckload of equally good merchandise packed inside ready to be offered the next day to customers with cash or a "good" check in hand.

As we all know, first glances can be deceiving.

A picker is an individual who often serves as a dealer's dealer. The picker must have knowledge about a broad spectrum of antiques and their current market values. The picker attends sales and auctions that sometimes are under advertised and held on a March morn-

ing in the rain. The picker's mission is often to buy the piece and "flip" it an hour or two days later with a markup that still leaves significant "room" for the next owner to make a profit.

The picker rolls the dice with some purchases. Usually there is a customer in mind and the price that the person will pay, but there are few guaranteed sales. The possibility of getting stuck with some unwanted merchandise is always there.

Let's put you in the position of the picker who has the opportunity to purchase the thirteen items illustrated in this section. You must evaluate and choose whether or not to buy the pieces for resale. After you have looked at the pictures, read the descriptions, "run" the numbers, select "buy it" or "don't buy it." After you have made your selections compare your reactions to our decisions and see how close we are to agreeing.

1. 3 gal. Midwestern crock, slip-tailed decoration, c. 1880-1900, excellent condition, price $95.

buy it   **don't buy it**

2. Butter bowl and butter worker, maple, factory-made, c. early 1900s, original condition, price $75 (both pieces).

buy it   **don't buy it**

3. Brass trumpet and case, c. 1915, playable, excellent condition, price $90.
buy it   **don't buy it**

5. Rolling pins, factory-made, maple, original condition, c. 1880-1920, price-$60 (both pins).
buy it   **don't buy it**

6. Copper apple butter kettle, late nineteenth century, iron handle, "as found" condition, 38" diameter, price $145.
buy it   **don't buy it**

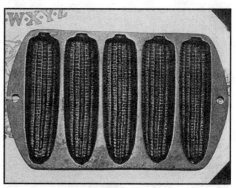

4. Spice chest, c. first quarter of the 20th century, refinished, original drawer pulls, excellent condition, price $145.
buy it   **don't buy it**

7. Cast iron corn muffin pan, original condition, c. 1920s, price-$25
buy it   **don't buy it**

8. Copper wash boiler, original lid, "as found" condition, c. early 1900s, price $45.

buy it   **don't buy it**

9. 1920s Babe Ruth Underwear box, excellent condition, price $225.

buy it   **don't buy it**

10. Wicker basket, "as found," c. twentieth century 20" diameter, structurally sound, price $52.

buy it   **don't buy it**

11. Podium from an Odd Fellows lodge, c. 1900-1925, oak, original finish, exceptional condition, price $200.

buy it   **don't buy it**

12. Unsigned oil painting from Maine, c. 1930s, excellent condition on canvas, price $100.

buy it   **don't buy it**

13. 2 gal. crock with Santa Claus face, 2 minor through lines from the rim, 9" tall, c. 1870; 1-1/2 gal. jar with lid, double flower decoration, excellent condition, 10" tall, c. 1870, price $2,200 (both pieces).

buy them   **don't buy them**

Our Decisions

1. There is probably another $45 (at least) in the price of this piece. As a picker, you could probably "flip" this reasonably quickly. It is not a great piece, but it is a "good" piece. Serious stoneware collectors would not be interested, but individuals who want a piece with a lot of "blue" would be.

2. At $75 there is not much of an opportunity for profit in these two pieces. We would pass.

3. Unless you had a specific buyer in mind, this might be difficult to unload profitably. We would pass. It also takes some knowledge about the instrument market and price structure which we don't have.

4. There is at least $100 left in the spice chest for resale. We would have liked it more if it maintained more of its original finish, but there are a lot of people who like "drawers" and are willing to pay for them.

5. There might be $10 or $15 left at this point, but we would still pass.

6. We would not be interested in this piece at any price. It is much too rough to our taste.

7. If you want to spend $25 to sell it for, $30-$35 it is a good buy.

8. The lid makes this an interesting piece and probably worth more than $45. We would attempt to sell this piece for about $75. The lid makes a $45 boiler worth $75.

9. The Ruth box is well worth the, $225, but it will not be an easy item to sell unless you know a serious baseball collector or an advertising collector. There is still a minimum of $100-$125 left in the Ruth box.

10. The wicker basket at $52 is overpriced.

11. The podium is in exceptional shape. It is the type of piece that can go from a shop to someone's front room but it may be semi-difficult to move at $250-$275. There is a growing interest in collecting lodge related items and an Odd Fellows collector may be interested in the piece or an oak collector. We would be much more interested in the piece at $100-$125 than the $200 asking price.

12. We don't know a great deal about paintings and would probably pass on this piece. A collector of automobile and gas station memorabilia might pay $200 for it, but we wouldn't know where to go with it.

13. There is potential here to make $800 on the two pieces of stoneware. Human faces are almost impossible to find, and Santa Claus has an additional obvious appeal. It will take a serious stoneware collector to buy these pieces and it may take some time to sell them both, but they are well worth the $2,200.

Glossary

The terms defined below are critical to your ability to function in the complex world of antiques and collectibles. It is essential that you memorize them and utilize each word in conversations with other devotees at least weekly.

Collectible: Refers to almost any item that was once popular for a minimum of two weeks.

Collectibles mall: The almost final resting place for the dredges of local garage sales and beanie babies with bent Ty tags and chipped Precious Moments.

"Early": To collectors of oak from Sears & Roebuck it's your grandmother's bedroom suite (sweet) and carnival glass.

"Early bird": The opportunity to pay $25-$100 to get into a show only after the dealers usually have had eight hours to "pick" it.

"Find": A significant purchase that you paid too much for and your spouse detests.

"Flip": The act of making a purchase, owning it for a brief period, and selling it for a quick profit. Many "finds" get "flipped" after a viewing by the non-buying spouse.

"Junior" country: A phrase that can be transposed with shabby chic to denote lesser quality examples of Americana that are especially popular in the Midwest.

Shabby chic: Furniture and accessories found curbside the night before the garbage truck comes down the street. Could be interchanged with "Junior" country.

CHAPTER 3

SHOPS, SHOWS, AUCTIONS, & GALLERIES

American Roots

A unique collection of early American country antiques can be found at American Roots, a multi-group shop located in the downtown historic district of Orange, California. American Roots specializes in original and early painted furniture, vintage textiles, decorated stoneware, toys and folk art. American Roots can be contacted at 105 W. Chapman Ave., Orange, CA 92666 and by telephone at (714) 639-3424. The shop is open 10 a.m. to 5 p.m. Monday through Saturday and from noon to 5 p.m. on Sunday.

Blacking box, $135; stoneware jar with stenciled decoration, $395.

Set of drawers, original painted finish, c. late nineteenth century, $750; "drop" handle boxes, $350 (each).

Yellowware baking bowl, c. 1920, $145.

Flag holder for a
bicycle, c. 1920, $125.

Steiff bear, c. 1907 with original
ear button, $1,200.

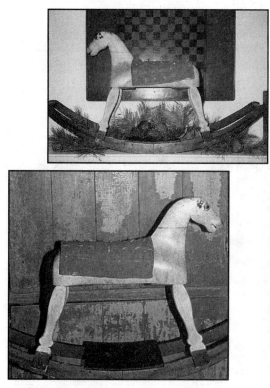

Rag doll with embroidered
face, c. 1880, clothes not
original to the doll, $295.

Nineteenth century horse on rocker with
original paint, $950.

Late nineteenth century boy rag doll,
original clothes, $195.

Turn-of-the-century "Berlin" work in original frame, $295.

Stoneware canning jars from Pennsylvania and West Virginia, nineteenth century, $165-$245 (each).

Horse hooked rug, c. 1930, $350.

Straw stuffed bear, 11" tall, original pads on feet, c. 1915-1920, $550.

Collection of early twentieth century tin child's alphabet plates, $185-$295.

Fabric art doll, c. 1900, small size, $125; fabric art cat, small, c. 1900, $55.

Papier-mâché rabbit container for candy holding spun cotton carrot in its mouth, glass eyes, c. 1915-20s, $165.

Oilcloth ball, c. 1920s-30s, $95; straw stuffed dog with shoe-button eyes, c. 1915-20, $95; stenciled red child's chair, early 1900s, $125.

Women's calico clothes, $195-$250 (each); drums, $125-295; flag stitchery, $295; bear, $350.

Nineteenth century hooked rug, $595; painted basket, $295; gathering basket (at left), $125.

Nineteenth century rag dolls, $500-$950 (each).

Black sock dolls, 8" tall, c. 1930, $250 (pair).

Steiff bear with button, $1,200; German jack-o-lantern, $155.

Hooked rug with horse's head, c. 1900, $650.

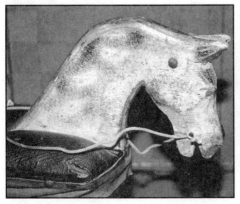

Dapple horse pull toy with leather coat, $395.

Child's blue calico clothes, $95-$135 (each).

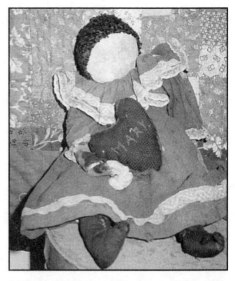

Steiff St. Bernard, $1,200; Steiff bear, $750.

Nineteenth century black rag doll, original clothes with drawn face, $250.

Painted pine dry sink, original painted finish, c. 1860, $1,450.

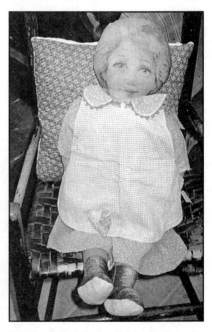

Early Raggedy Ann & Andy dolls, $1,200 (each).

Fabric art doll, c. 1900, clothes not original to the doll, $225.

Painted white table, pine, single drawer, $400-475; yellowware bowl with white band, $85-100; small stack of three pantry boxes, $400-$450.

Small Steiff bear, $1,100.

Bear, $350; flag holder, $125; doll quilt, $95.

Nineteenth century game board, $495; antique sign, $595; cloth ball, $95.

Aston Macek Auction Company

The pictures and prices that follow were provided by the Aston Macek Auction Company of Endwell, New York. The profusely illustrated Aston Macek catalogs have won awards from the New York State Auctioneers' Association. There is no charge to be placed on their mailing list.

Aston Macek is also holding auctions "live" on the Internet at eBay, the world's largest auction site which can be reached at www.ebay.com and Aston Macek can be found under the seller category as "folkman2."

Aston Macek Auction Company can be reached at
2825 Country Club Road
Endwell, NY 13760
Telephone: 607-785-6598
E-mail: folkman2.stny.lrun.com

All prices include a 10% buyer's premium.

Pa. farm table in early grey over original brown paint, scrubbed 3-board pinned top, c. 19th century, $1,595.

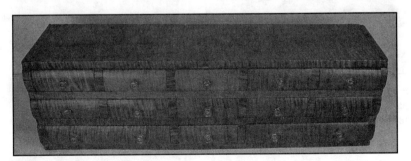

Highly figured tiger maple set of 13 drawers, American, c. early nineteenth century, $2,035.

Large hand carved burl bowl with cutout handles c. 18th century, probably Iroquois, $2,420.

Group of three "flattie" shorebirds on bases in original condition, $264.

Shaker table swift, Hancock, MA, c. 1850, $264; possibly Shaker bucket/crock bench in red with half-moon cutout base & 4 shelves, $880; Shaker #7 rocker with Mt. Lebanon label, tape seat, possible restoration, $715.

Pair of Pennsylvania paint decorated chairs with painted angel wing crests & bluebird accented seats, $577.50 (pair).

Watercolor & ink drawing with bird on branch & early rhymed verse, framed, $475.

Lancaster Co. PA dough bin in original blue/black surface, dovetailed box with hand planed tapered legs, $742.50; large oval bentwood band box with graining & floral paint, $1,265.

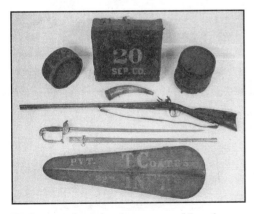

Early staved rumlet or canteen with red, possibly Maine in origin, $132; violin case, $467.50; flintlock fowler, $275; Confederate canteen, $743.

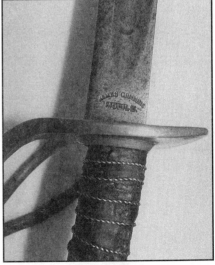

James Connine (Mobile) Confederate cavalry saber, once owned by Leroy S. Tidwell of the 39th Georgia Regiment, $13,750.

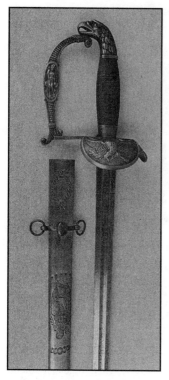

American eagle head sword, etched blade, eagle and US on scabbard, $962.50.

Classic 18th century American Chippendale easy chair, New England, stretcher-less with serpentine wings & rolled arms, retaining its original finish & original linen, $1,850.

Rare form early burl storage box with lift out sectioned tray, $1,980.

Civil War era painted decorated "Washington Guards" drum with spread winged eagle & other decorations, $3,600.

Shaker Bentwood covered oval pantry box, cherry stain, $225; two-piece Shaker herb grinder, carved-out wooden base & turned wood grinding wheel, $675; classic Shaker table top flour sifter, $375.

Significant historical coverlet with eagle & Independence Hall border, dated 1840, attributed to James Cunningham, $800.

PA German bride's box, $1,300.

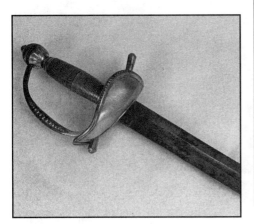

Sword presented to Confederate General Stevenson upon his graduation from West Point in 1838, $8,000.

Cased 1862 Police Colt in excellent condition with 5.5" barrel, includes powder flask, bullet mold, percussion caps, bullets & ball, $6,500.

Rarely found redware slip cup, brown glaze & pouring spout for goose quill, $3,550; earthenware slip cup, wheel thrown, brown glaze & pouring spout for goose quill, New York state origin, $420.

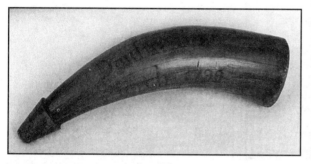

Power horn inscribed with 13 star flag & rifle signed "L. C. Paul, Carsonville, Daufin Co., March, 1799", PA origin, $1,225.

Pair of early folk carved dog's heads furniture crests, from a Hudson River estate, $1,000.

Silas Hoadley 30-hour tall case clock with Thomas & Hoadley wooden works, c. 1810-1813, pine case stained mahogany, central eagle finial replacement, $1,450.

Small Shaker storage box with two swallowtail fingers & great crackled salmon paint, copper nails, $625.

Rare Native American tin quilt pattern from Lehighton, PA, $1,550.

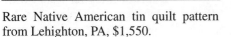

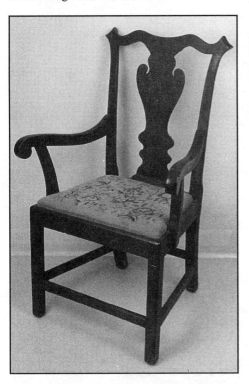

Ohio Mennonite gathering basket with unusual wooden bottom signed "Eli", $675.

Conservative & sturdy Philadelphia mahogany armchair in the Chippendale style, attributed to William Savery, $1,200.

Stephen Van Rensselaer burl snuff box, New York's first Lt. Gov., $850.

Rare double eagle chip carved butter print, pine, New England or Pennsylvania origin, $450.

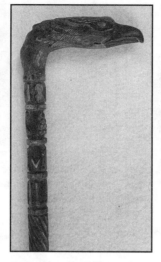

Folk carved Civil War era cane with eagle's head grip, shaft signed "RIV1" (First Rhode Island Volunteers) dated 1863, $1,400.

Excellent coin silver teapot with "R" monogram, attributed to the Randolph family of Virginia, $2,200.

Excellent early American screw top adjustable candlestand with floral paint decoration on dish, faint original stencil remnants, $2,500.

Two tiered Shaker bucket bench in early white surface, $2,000; Shaker oval swing handled carrier labeled "Alfred Maine/ Shaker Goods", $90; Shaker #7 bonnet, c. mid-nineteenth century, $90.

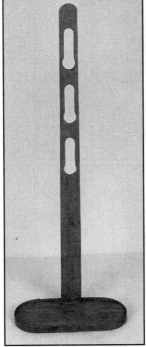

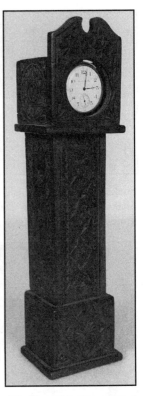

Queen Anne heart & crown sidechair, American, probably Guilford, CN, c. 1740-1770, $1,300.

Rare Shaker two candle hanging sconce, probably Pleasant Hill, KY, early to mid-nineteenth century, $1,750.

Finely Friesian-carved & nicely proportioned walnut watch hutch in tall case form, $550.

Shaker pin cushion, $110; wrought iron and brass Shaker skimmer, $140; Shaker thermometer in turned wooden case, $150; rare miniature Shaker mirror, $220.

Hand painted KPM cup & saucer, c. 1780-1800, $1,250.

Shaker firkin signed "Elder Clark", $400; Shaker hearth broom, $200; Shaker herb grinder, $100.

Shaker tin colander, $115; Shaker tin syrup, $80; Shaker maple sugar mold, $130; rare Shaker tin coffee pot, $140.

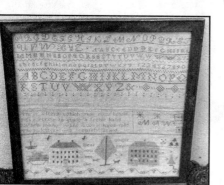

Fine York County, PA linen sampler dated 1834, $1,900.

Bliss-style 3 piece train set, $1,500; Bliss-style Victorian era "row" house, $1,200.

Chester County, PA Chippendale slant-top desk, walnut with bold ogee bracket feet, early or original finish, 4 graduated drawers retaining most of original rosette & bail handles, $5,000.

Rare Shaker sorting chair, Mt. Lebanon, NY, mid-1800s, $850.

Early cutout & dovetailed candle sconce in salmon-bittersweet paint, probably from New Hampshire, $950.

Shaker 3 tier pagoda form sewing tree, $200; Shaker "Apostle" trivet, $55; Shaker string winder, $220.

Folk carved & painted horse on painted decorated wooden platform, $950.

Early Spring Farm Antiques

Martha's Vineyard, an island seven miles from Woods Hole, Cape Cod, is rich in history. The island was named in 1602 and is probably best known for its whaling industry, camp meeting gingerbread cottages, and its charming villages and towns.

Like so many vacation spots, the island population changes from 17,000 to 60,000 winter and summer. The Wampanog Indians, the first inhabitants, made pottery from the clay cliffs at Gay Head and also wove baskets.

There are many antiques on Martha's Vineyard and shops in all of the towns. A good many of the antiques at Early Spring Farm are from island homes with local history.

My barn is right behind our house where I have the shop. I also sell furniture from the Women's Co-op, a store full of quality Vineyard-made crafts. My furniture is used to display the locally made pottery, weaving quilts, and paintings.

A twice weekly flea market in a Chilmark church yard is very popular during the summer. The 35 minute boat ride from the mainland is well worth the effort for visitors interested in the natural bounty and beauty of our island where antique treasures are still to be found.

Allan & Linc Hanson
Early Spring Farm Antiques
RR 2, Box 1A
93 Lagood Pond Road
Vineyard Haven, MA 02568-9701

Nineteenth century dome top cupboard, grain painted, $990.

New England fan back Windsor chair, c. 1800, $500.

Small barn cupola, early twentieth century, $195.

Neat two sided bird house, red, black, early twentieth century, $185.

Martha's Vineyard chest in original paint, c. 1880, $500.

Two game boards, red & black; small board, $260; large board, $225.

Folksy doll house in old paint, $298.

Family of teddy bears, $125-$225.

Charming three step advertising piece, lithographed tin back, $300.

Child-size cottage chest, c. 1860, $325.

Early 1900s hooked rug, $300.

Child-size cottage chest, original painted decoration, $498.

Slat Canadian goose, $125; "Mary Lou" boat, $245.

Large wooden sign from Mass., $398.

Early twentieth century hooked rug, $375.

Folk art diorama from Martha's Vineyard, c. 1970, $300.

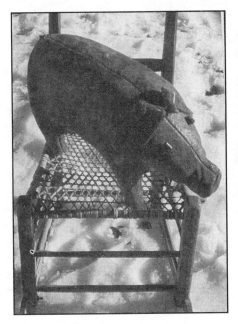

Collection of early 1900s signs, $50-$150.

"Babe" c. 1920 footstool, $250.

Copake Auction, Inc.

Michael and Seth Fallon are auctioneers and appraisers who conduct scheduled monthly cataloged Americana auctions of formal, country, and Victorian furniture, period accessories, quilts, textiles, folk art, tramp art, art work, and more. Each year, the Copake Auction also conducts the, "best bicycle sale in the world," featuring antique bicycles and related memorabilia. Recently, the Copake Auction has begun conducting annual chintz china auctions each spring. The Fallon's are members of numerous state and national associations for auctioneers. The items that follow have been sold recently at Copake Auction. For more information: Copake Auction, Inc., PO Box H, Copake, NY 12516, (518) 329-1142, fax (518) 329-3369, email: infor@copakeauction.com, web site: www.copakeauction.com

The Copake Auction is located in Columbia County, NY off of Route 22, with easy access from the Taconic State Parkway.

Rhode Island porringer top tea table, $29,700.

One of a 3-piece carved and inlaid oak set consisting of partner's desk and two matching "kas" style cabinets, $10,175 (set of 3 pieces).

Nineteenth century Hepplewhite cupboard with original surface, $7,150.

Great Barrington sampler, $2,970.

Nineteenth century Biedermeier pole type firescreen, $1,875.

Blue bill drake decoy signed by both the Ward brothers, $10,450.

Nineteenth century beaded purse, $935.

Nineteenth century Civil War drum labeled "Stephen Emory Rindge, N.Y.", $2,530.

Spectacular hooked rug depicting animals and people, $4,400.

Nineteenth century watercolor depicting women and young girls, $2,650.

Folk art velocipedge rider (ex Roger Johnson collection), $4,200.

Late nineteenth century cow weathervane, copper, traces of original gilding, $4,675.

Great Barrington, Mass. watercolor depicting views of a town landmark, $2,090.

Native American buffalo robe, c. 1860-1880, from the Mandan tribe of South Dakota, $5,500.

Eighteenth century oil on canvas, Italian school painting of a canal scene, $4,125.

Tramp art diorama of a sailing ship, $1,760.

Nineteenth century copper ewe weather-vane, $2,860.

C. 1930s pedal car, $1,320.

Pair of early iron garden gates, $3,200.

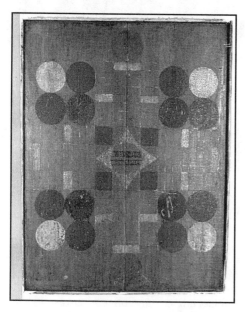

Two sided game board, $2,650.

Dough bin in original blue paint, unusual form, $1,100.

"Memory style" stamp art frame, $4,950.

Tall 5-drawer chest in mustard paint over original red surface, c. 1790-1810, $3,575.

Victorian oak crystal cabinet having arched top with North Wind God carvings on front with bell flowers, $4,400.

Nineteenth century Quebecois butternut inlaid cabinet, $3,190.

Architectural medicine cabinet, $2,200.

Late nineteenth century jelly cupboard in vinegar grain paint, $2,475.

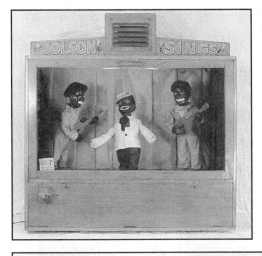

Circa 1920-40 arcade coin-op auctioma-
tion "Jolson Sings", $2,090.

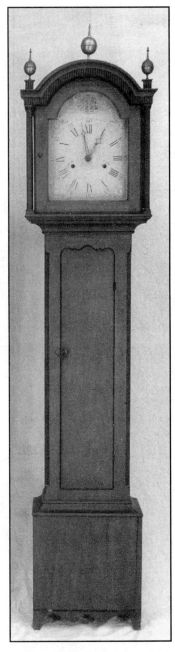

Pair of Heywood Wakefield chairs, $2,200.

Pine apothecary chest, 46-drawer, nineteenth
century, $3,080.

Hopkins & Lewis Litchfield,
Conn., tall case clock, $5,500.

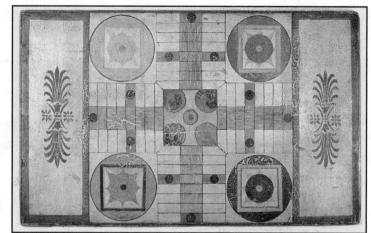

Two-sided game board, $5,500.

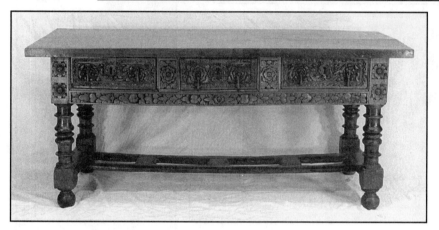

Seventeenth century Spanish refractory table, $3,850.

Hepplewhite sideboard, $12,650.

Baker & Company Antiques

Baker & Company Antiques opened in Soquel, California in 1997. Soquel is a circa 1860 picturesque village located on the Monterey Bay near Santa Cruz about halfway between San Francisco and Monterey/Carmel. Although the shop is relatively new, the dealers involved have each been in Americana business for many years. The dealers are Tom Baker, Judie Dilworth, Mary Lou & John Finnigan, Jim Livesey, and Kathey Sarr. Each dealer specializes in different areas of early American antiques. As a group they have over 100 years of experience in collecting and dealing in early Americana. In addition to the shop, Baker & Company has an active web site at: http://www.BakerCoAntiques.com.

Baker & Company can be contacted at:

5011 Soquel Drive
Soquel, CA 95073
831-479-4404

Pine doll dresser, 19th century, $250; pine doll pewter cupboard, 19th century, $395; miniature chest, 5 drawers, 18th century, $795.

Spongeware pitcher with flower design, $600; pine doll pewter cupboard, 19th century, $350; spongeware milk pan, $265.

Late 19th century hooked rug, $750-$950.

Grouping of tin, iron and brass lighting, some in original paint, 18th to mid 19th century, $150-$450 each.

Student's lamp, nickel over brass, late 1800s, $695.

Iron toaster, rare, 18th century, $425.

Brass candlestick (left) from Spain, circa 1710, $295; brass candlestick (right), English Queen Ann style, circa 1740, $225.

Staffordshire Spaniel, 19th century, $295.

Pair mid-drip candlesticks (left), Dutch, circa 1650, $1,200; pair Spanish candlesticks (right), 16th century, $1,200.

Brass candle snuffer & tray, 18th century, $195; brass candlestick, Queen Ann, 18th century, $195.

Pewter candlesticks (left), circa 1840; English, $250; pewter candlesticks (right), 18th century, $1,200.

19th century peaseware, $200-$500 each.

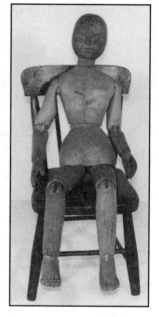

Doll in salesman's sample high chair, $600; doll high chair, $1,000.

19th century scrub box in original blue paint with brush, $950.

Peg wooden doll, 19th century, $600.

Penny rug, mid 19th century, $400-$450.

19th century American game boards in original paint, from left: rare grain painted Ringo with checkerboard in reverse side, $1,950; fox and geese with checkerboard on reverse side, $450; Chinese checkers, $475.

19th century American game boards in original paint, from left: miniature folding checkerboard and Mill Game, Backgammon on reverse side, $950; folding 6-color game board, Backgammon inside, checkerboard outside, $850; signed checkerboard with pinstriping, $900; red/black/mustard checkerboard with slide-top compartment underneath with original painted wooden checkers, $1,450; checkerboard with the Mill Game on reverse side, $1,250.

19th century American game boards in original paint, from left: ring toss, $250; spinning, $200; 5-color Parcheesi, $1,250; cribbage, $225; fox and geese, $275.

Civil War watercolor, $1,500-$1,750.

Eagle shooting gallery target, original polychrome paint, signed "A.J. Smith, Chicago," $950.

Jerome "OG" shelf clock, 8-day, weight, dates 1854, $795.

Seth Thomas cottage clock, 30-hour, circa 1856, $795.

William F. Gilbert jewelers clock, 8-day, 65 in., circa 1895-1910, $7,500.

Charles Kirk, pillar & scroll clock, cherry, 30-hour, dates 1827, $5,500.

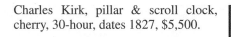

New Haven rare 60-day banjo clock, 42-inch, late 1800s, $2,500.

Seth Thomas walnut No. 1 parlor calendar clock, 8-day, circa 1863, $3,500.

Scared kitty doorstop in original paint, c. 1880, $325-$350.

Chalkware lamb, original paint, early to mid 19th century, $650; redware pig, original paint, early to mid 19th century, $750.

All mid 19th century (left to right): splint basket in original blueberry paint, probably Shaker, $800-$1,200; rare tin candleholder with mid-drip, original blue paint, $395; swing handle splint basket with demi-John bottom, $250-$350.

Painted & decorated box, circa 1860, $695.

Wagon seat in original red paint and pin-striping, mid 19th century, $350-$400.

Rare American sampler, signed and dated "1845" with Hebrew Alphabet and homespun binding, New Jersey origin, $2,000-$2,500.

Sampler dated 1792, wrought by Betsy Thurston, $895.

Signed Butternut trencher with stone fruit, $350; stone fruit and stone nuts, $35-$95 each.

Unmarked stoneware, mid 19th century: 1/2 gallon crock attributed to Edmonds, Charlestown, Mass., $450; 1/2 gallon jug, deep cobalt design, $495.

Tin wall candle sconce, crimped holder, traces of original paint, 18th century, $450; toleware match safe, original paint, c. 1840, $275.

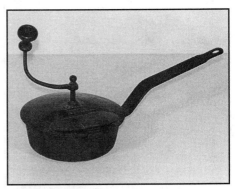

Iron chestnut roaster, 19th century, $150-$175.

Stack of painted Shaker oval fingered boxes, 19th century, $750-$1,600 each.

Stack of original paint decorated wooden boxes, early 19th century, from top: mustard, $350; black, $750; mustard, $400; green, $470; red, $850; carved baleen box with painted carved wooden top, $2,500-$3,000; carved gunwood box, original painted snake pops out when slide top is opened, $650-$850; original painted green tin candle snuffer, $75-$95.

Early 19th century 2-tiered wallbox in original red paint, $2,500-$3,000; 19th century butter stamps: eagle, $395; thistle, $195; acorn & leaves, $200; sheaf of wheat, $225.

Sandwich glass compote, $75; with strawberry emeries, 19th century, $25-$125 each.

Simply Country Antiques Show

The Simply Country Antiques Show was started and is managed by Carolyn Stone and Kathy Hind. It grew out of a need to fill a void in the Pacific Northwest for a quality Americana and country antiques show. Simply Country draws approximately 50 dealers to each show from Washington, Oregon, Idaho, Montana, California, New York, New Mexico, Illinois, and Canada. The show is held twice a year, the last weekend in March (unless it falls on Easter) and the last weekend in September at Overlake School, a private school in Redmond, Washington.

The address of the Simply Country Show is:

20301 N.E. 108th St.
Redmond, Washington 98052
Telephone: 425-556-9336

There is free parking and no early bird admission. The show hours are 10 a.m.-7 p.m. on Saturday and 11 a.m.-5 p.m. on Sunday.

Oil on canvas, c. 1830-1840, portrait of gentleman, Pennsylvania or New England in origin (Iron Eagle-Newport, Ore.), $7,500.

Bannister-back chair in old dry red-brown paint, replaced seat, $750.

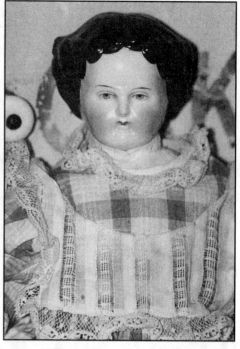

China doll, 14", c. 1860-70 (Smith & Jones Antiques, Redmond, WA), $450.

China doll, c. 1860, 14"-16" (Smith & Jones Antiques), $495.

Nineteenth century sailor's valentine, seashells, $2,800. Nineteenth century sailer's string basket (Iron Eagle), $195.

1940s English pub sign for Bass Ale, $375.

Grained jelly cupboard from Pennsylvania,
c. 1850, $1,250.

Mid-nineteenth century Mennonite blanket chest on legs, original painted surface,
$795.

Early nineteenth century open top cupboard, red paint (Nantucket NW), $3,200.

Pastel portrait of gentleman, c. 1840s, Tilton, NH (Judy Knowles Antiques, Salem, OR), $1,500.

Blue cupboard, c. late nineteenth century (Judy Knowles Antiques), $225.

Theorem, c. 1860, watercolor on paper, $2,200.

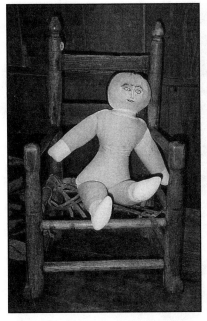

Early eighteenth century German Stoneard tankard made from the English market, $350; pearlware pitcher with some damage, $195; assorted pincushions, $45 (each).

Mid-nineteenth century child's rocker, $110; rag doll (Nantucket NW, Molalla, OR), $250.

Tiger maple cobbler's bench (JK Antiques, Kirkland, WA), $595.

Mid 1800s grained checkerboard-top table, all original from Mass. (Greenfield Antiques, San Anselmo, CA), $1,900.

Nineteenth century pie safe with original hearts, 8 stars, tins, later grained paint, $1,500.

Mennonite dry sink, c. 1830-40 original painted finish (Nancy B. Cooper Antiques, San Francisco), $2,400.

Three nineteenth century bandboxes and a beaver hat (left to right), $175; $325; $500.

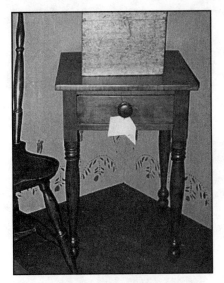

Cherry stand (Aaberg Antiques, Port-land, OR), $495.

Assortment of early cookie cutters mounted on old cutting board, $2,000.

Assorted American pewter teapots (Mackay Antiques, Los Altos Hills, California), $200-$450 each.

Nineteenth century oil portrait (Aaberg Antiques), $1,200.

Child's Windsor chair in blue-green paint (Mackay Antiques), $350.

Goat or pony cart, c. 1930 (Mackay Antiques), $550.

Chippendale mirror, $360; 18th century silk on silk embroidery, $1,550; Lucy Barlow sampler, NH, c. 1811, $1,150; stoneware bird jug with strong cobalt decoration (Hickory Hill Antiques, Bothwell, WA), $895.

Gaff-rigged pond sailor, c. 1930 (Furytown Antiques, Mendocino, CA), $1,195.

Basket of flowers hooked rug (Baker & Company, Soquel, CA), $850.

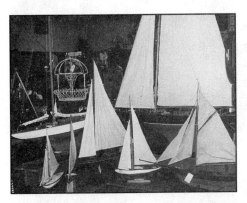

Assorted American pond boats (Furytown Antiques), $125-$2,400.

Basket of flowers wool stitchery, c. 1840s, $950.

Victorian child's horse & cart, original condition (Patina, Seattle, WA), $4,000.

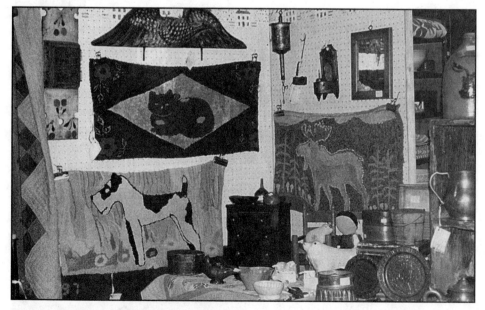

Cat hooked rug, $550; Scotty dog, $275; moose, $650 (Greenfield, San Anselmo, CA).

Babyland rag doll, early face underneath with later face on top, 32", $995.

Child's painted sled with horse decoration, $995.

Large New England potato stamp basket with lid, c. 1840s, $500.

Hooked gloves with heart motif (Lori Brooks, Seattle, WA), $395.

Pillar & scroll clock, c. 1840-1850, $1,500.

Two blue wallpaper bandboxes, nineteenth century (Greenfield Antiques); large box, $710; small box, $350.

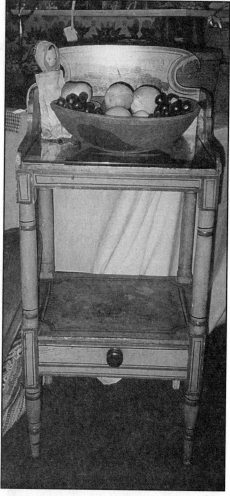

Sheraton painted decorated washstand, original paint & decoration, c. 1820 (Greenfield Antiques), $375.

American pond sailor with original maker's label "Tex Johnson, New York" (Hickory Hills Antiques), $695.

Red hanging pin cupboard, Pennsylvania, original red wash, $425; walnut dough box, Pennsylvania, original brown paint, $975; Cobalt decorated stoneware, $395-$695 (Hickory Hill Antiques, Bothwell, WA).

Silk on silk embroidery entitled "Hope," c. 1820 14-1/2" x 16-1/2" (Greenfield Antiques), $1,700.

Bowl of fruit theorem on velvet, 15" x 17", c. 1830s (Greenfield Antiques), $2,000.

Unusual piece of framed needlework (Greenfield Antiques), $800.

Hooked rug, great large size geometric with floral inner boarder (Gary Holt Collection, Missoula MT), $2,500.

Theorem on velvet, tilted bowl of fruit, c. 1830 (Greenfield Antiques), $2,400.

Two drawer stand with drop leaves, tiger maple drawer fronts, original brass pulls, c. 1820 (Furytown Antiques), $1,200.

Sampler dated 1824 (Greenfield Antiques), $1,600.

Sophia Nickerson's sampler, dated 1841 (Chelsea Antiques, Seattle), $650.

Hooked rug in brown tones with three horses (Baker & Company), $995.

Hooked rug with birds (Greenfield Antiques), $600.

Bandbox, c. 1830s, 13" high x 17" long x 11" across (Greenfield Antiques), $850.

Wallpaper band box in mustard, brown & green, c. 1830 (Greenfield Antiques), $675.

Country federal mirror, c. 1800, $475; pearlware pitcher (some damage), $195; rag doll, $800 (Nantucket NW, Molella, OR).

Assorted papier-mâché roly polys (Treasure Valley), $125-$650 each.

Silk and watercolor silk memorial, encircled with braided hair band, c. 1820-25, 19-1/2" x 20-1/2", $2,400.

Floral theorem, c. 1830s-40s, watercolor on velvet (Judy Knowles Antiques, Salem, OR), $1,800.

Chippendale dropleaf table, c. 1780 (Frank Tichy, Coupeville, WA), $3,600.

Liberty Tree Antiques

Liberty Tree Antiques specializes in American country antiques in early paint including furniture, painted smalls, quilts, samplers, toys and folk art. We are located in the town of Collierville, TN just 20 miles east of Memphis. The shop is open Wednesday through Saturday 10 AM till 4 PM or any time by appointment. A call ahead is advised if coming from a long distance. For more information, contact Liberty Tree Antiques, 120 North Main Street, Collierville, TN 38017, (901) 854-4364 or (901) 853-3531.

Pennsylvania wood box-bench in original red finish, $1,200.

Meal bin from Maine, original green paint, $995.

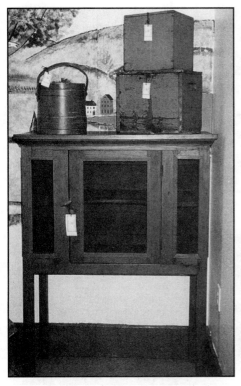

Early step-back cupboard in original red paint, $3,000.

Screened pie safe in red wash, $995; painted wood boxes, $150 (each).

Screened pie safe, $1,200.

Leather fire bucket, dated 1852, $1,200.

Corner cupboard with mustard paint, $1,200.

Realty agency sign, $550.

Wooden trencher bowl, $295; hogscraper candlesticks, $175 (each for the tall examples); $150 (for the others).

Bride's box, $650.

Trade sign in the shape of a pocket watch, double-sided wood and iron, $695.

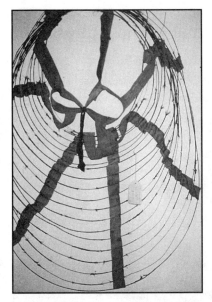

Ladies hoop skirt hoop, patented 1852, $150.

Step-back cupboard in green over darker green, $2,000.

Carved tin trade from carpet weaver, $450.

Countertop store drawers in red paint, $750.

Ohio dry sink in powder blue paint, $1,200.

Hand colored lithographed store poster in red frame, $550.

Nineteenth century Pennsylvania watercolor with some water damage, $695.

Sophia Waite's sampler from 1847, $650.

Potato seed cutter in original red paint, $295.

Buttery cupboard from an old house in New Hampshire, $3,500.

Plantation type desk in early finish, $2,000.

Nine drawer chest in mustard paint, $3,500.

Original blue painted spinning wheel, $900.

Red, white, & blue basket quilt, $395.

Hanging spice box in green and red, $795.

Assorted glass apothecary jars, $195-$225 (each). Straw stuffed tiger, $250.

Stack of wallpaper bandboxes, $195-$550 (each).

Pennsylvania blanket chest in original blue paint, dated 1839, $950.

Jane Sargent's sampler dated 1829, $450.

Maine Baking Co. sign on stretched canvas, $550; Dr. R. Laurence sign, $295.

Doris Stauble millinery arrangement in antique bandbox, $395.

Cafe sign, $295.

Sea captain's desk in old finish, $2,000.

Step back cupboard with pie shelf and original grain painted finish, $3,500.

Theorem painting of cat by artist William Rank, $350.

New England clerk's desk, c. 1850, original red paint, $1,500.

Six tin pie safe in original blue paint, $2,500.

Hudson River Valley step-back cupboard with early green & cream paint, $2,500.

Open front cupboard in old blue paint, $1,200; red log cabin quilt, $350.

42-drawer apothecary in mustard and red paint, $2,000.

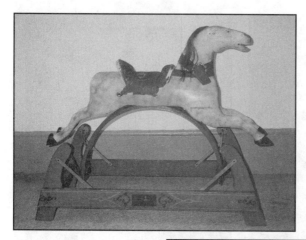

Rocking horse, $895.

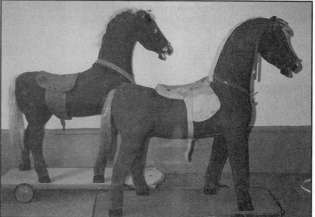

Two horse pull toys covered in brown burlap, $595 each.

Nineteenth century chintz quilt, bird of paradise pattern, some staining and wear, $2,000.

Collectors' Choice Antique Gallery

Twenty-five years ago, there were numerous communities in the east and Midwest that featured a multitude of quality antiques shops within their corporate limits. It was possible to spend a day in these towns walking from shop to shop and actually finding a number of things to buy from knowledgeable dealers. Most of these shops have been turned into Pier One outposts and coffee houses with stale graham crackers dipped in waxy chocolate.

New Oxford, Pennsylvania is one of the few antiques-oriented communities that have survived and prospered with numerous quality shops, malls, and galleries with a general emphasis on Americana. New Oxford is located near York and Gettysburg and is the home of one of our favorite antiques establishments, the Collectors' Choice Antique Gallery.

Andrea Hollenbaugh serves as gallery director at Collectors' Choice which has about 85 dealers displaying their merchandise. The gallery offers an exciting variety of country and period furniture and the best in accessories, including yellowware, pearlware, mocha, iron, toys, dolls, firearms and accouterments, sewing items, antique jewelry, textiles, ephemera, paintings and portraits.

Collectors' Choice may be reached at:

330 Golden Lane, New Oxford, PA 17350

(717) 624-3440

The gallery is open from 10 a.m. to 5 p.m. Monday through Saturday, and noon to 5 p.m. on Sunday, or by special appointment and ships almost anything anywhere.

Miniature Empire chest with flame mahogany veneer, $1,295.

New England portraits, 33-1/4" x 18-1/4", c. 1830, $4,850.

MD or VA country mahogany server c. 1810, $3,250.

Lancaster, PA tiger maple paint grained sliding lid candlebox w/drawer 12-1/2" x 6", $1,950.

William Bowyer London 30-hr. Langern clock, $8,800.

Magnificent Masonic frame, 48" x 31", $1,150.

Collection of one full-body and leg calipers ranging from, $160-$495.

18th century shoe buckles, value from $325-$375 (pair).

Unusual nurse's chatelaine $600; three wonderful eyeglass chatelaines, $175-$475.

Curly maple hanging dovetailed utility box, $560; upholstered Windsor stool/brn. & white fabric top, $130.

Bliss stable c. 1900, 16-1/2" wide x 8" deep, $1,395.

Exciting "Ellinger" rooster painting on velvet, $2,600.

Lidded basketweave blue & white stoneware "Coffee" cannister, $275; Flow Blue "Rhone" reticulated tray, $825; mint black & white banded mocha tankard, $325.

Rare Washington Centennial plate (1871-1903), $525; yellowware "Sugar" canister w/blue, grn., brn. Sponge, 7-1/4" tall, $225; pr. American 19th century candlesticks w/brown sponge on yellowware backing, $950.

Queen's Rose toddy plate, $300; Clews "Water Girl" 1820s dark blue pitcher, $490; Lehnware egg cup w/strawberry & vine dec., $450.

Advertising tins: Mrs. Dinsmore's Cough Drops, $300; Rough Rider baking powder, $110; Simon's Roosevelt tobacco tin, $170.

Inlaid cutlery box w/heart, $850; vibrant watercolor of little girl in blue dress signed, "Wybrant 1849," $895.

18th century wax profile, $850; 18th century bird needlework on paper, "Red Pole 1794," $1,100.

Cobalt blue sugar basin w/honeycomb pat., $950; medium blue open salt, $475; cobalt blue bottle-Connecticut, $530.

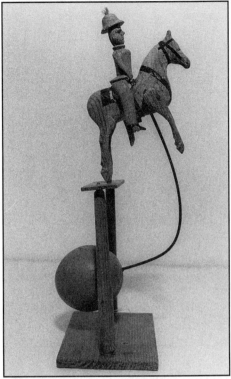

Early carved wood horse & rider balance toy, $1,800.

"Hubbard" full-bodied silhouettes, $650 each; "Pearce" 1895 full-bodies silhouette of young man, $515.

Dutch silver chatelaine, c. 1880, $1,140; complete enameled chatelaine, $925; 3 figural cigar cutters, $95-$335.

American walnut min. inlaid chest of drawers, $1,350.

Kentucky punched tin pie safe w/front tins "W. Jones", $1,900.

Miniature step back cupboard, c. 1870, $1,450; miniature ice box pat. 1874, "The Colorado Refrigerator," Easton, PA, $2,500.

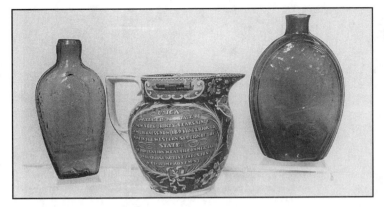

Masonic green flask, $475; dark blue pitcher, Erie Canal-DeWitt Clinton Eulogy, $1,725; olive color Washington/Jackson flask, $225.

Blue and red spatter sugar bowl w/lid, $650; Great Earthworm mocha bowl w/grn. top, $2,950.

Yellowware parrot bank, $450; blue mocha pitcher w/cable dec., $695; yellowware fruit mold, American, $375.

Sydenham ironstone sm. gravy tureen, $275; Ceres Wheat ironstone sauce tureen, $200; Wheat & Blackberry ironstone soup, $300.

Pfaltzgraff, York, PA 13" stoneware jug, $550; New Jersey stoneware pitcher, $395.

Kewpie dishes (right) large plate, $215; Kewpie creamer (middle), $155; Kewpie bowl (top left), $145; Kewpie plate (bottom left), $170.

Blown 3-mold 5-1/4" flip, $280; "Smocking" pattern glass sugar & creamer, $290; Ashburton quart size flip, $175.

Double Rose Gaudy Dutch 10" plate $1,250; Sailor's Farewell pink lustre bowl $1,850; Leeds type blue feather edge plate w/rare five-color floral decoration, $950.

9-1/4" slip dec. redware plate, $465; 11-1/4" redware food mold w/oven patina, $465; redware covered sugar bowl, $925.

Early pewter porringer initialed "R.G.", $375; Pilgrim century chip-carved walnut mirror, $1,450; sm. early folksy frame, "Blanch" on front, $330.

19th century bearded man w/pointed cap nutcracker, $325; 20th century full-bodied peasant woman $285; 19th century ornately carved Chinese man in sitting position, $395.

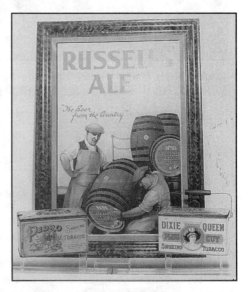

Russell's Ales sign, $575; Pedro cut plug tin $85; Dixie Queen plug cut in, $265.

Set of four Sheraton Tiger Maple side chairs w/cane seats, $1,600.

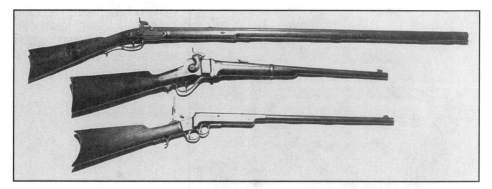

"J. Pritz" PA "Kentucky," Hanover, PA, $2,100; Sharps "New Model" 1863 conversion, $2,200, 3rd Model, Frank Wesson rim fire, $625.

PA Dower chest from Berks/Lebanon Counties, c. 1785, $16,000.

Burl butter paddle 8" tall, $485; burl footed bowl with molded edge, 6-1/4", $765; burl footed bowl, 10-1/4", $825.

Wedgewood Whieldon-type emerald grn. Strainer, c. 1760, $300; emerald green earthenware bowl, $1,450; rare form, blue edge tray, $205.

Yellowware mug depicting farming & hunting motifs, $1,825; lg. yellowware mug w/classical motifs, $925; blue Seawood pattern yellowware cup, $435.

Eureka Steam Laundry
sign, c. 1915, $500-$600.

Odd Fellows' podium, c.
early 1900s, $2,000-$3,000.

Odd Fellows "heart
in hand," c. 1900,
$1,500-$2,000.

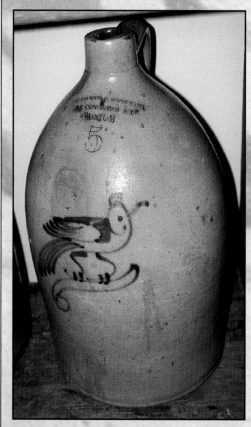

**Six gallon stoneware jug with bird,
$450-$550.**

Baskets, $250-$900 each.

Rare stone fruit apple with stone leaf, $800-$900.

Late stone fruit, $20-$25.

Stone fruit collection, $5,600.

Bisque head acrobat with rare weights, $500-$600.

Bisque head Schoenhut acrobat, $350.

Felt pennants, c. 1930s-1940s, $35-$45.

1950 child's baseball uniform, $35-$50.

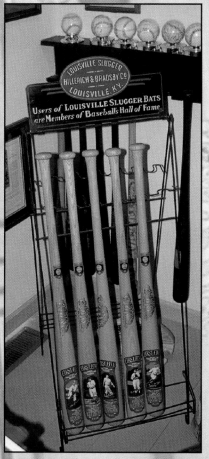

1915 Federal League doll, $1,000-$1,500.

Rare 1939 bat rack, $1,000-$1,500.

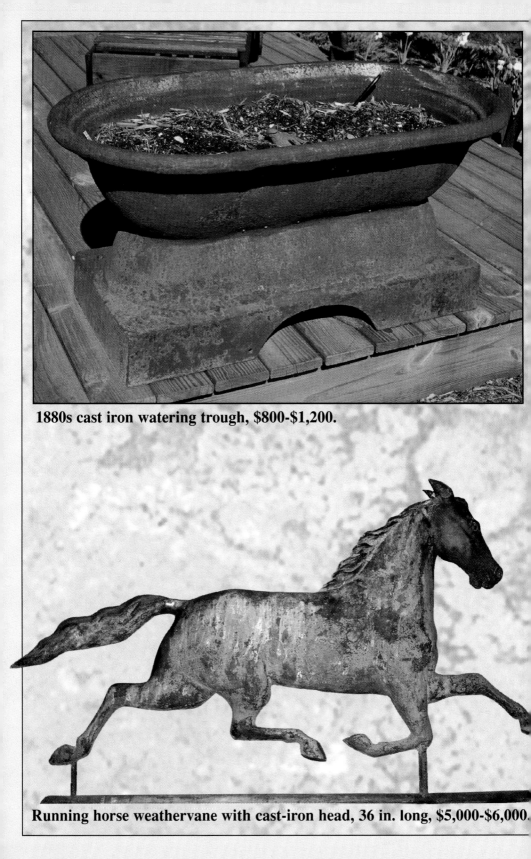

1880s cast iron watering trough, $800-$1,200.

Running horse weathervane with cast-iron head, 36 in. long, $5,000-$6,000.

"Prison" made hickory chair, c. 1940, $475-$575.

Old Hickory 6 ft. settee, c. 1930, $3,000-$3,500.

Straw filled Santa dolls, German, c. 1930s, $225-$350 each.

7 ft. tall feather tree, c. 1915, $1,000-$1,500.

Pot Pourri

The items that follow were photographed in shops and at shows from Illinois to Pennsylvania and Maine. The values reported are retail and were taken directly from the price tags. We made every effort to ensure that the piece was in at least "good" condition, structurally sound, and with an original or painted surface.

Copper candy kettles, 18" and 24" diameters, iron handles, early twentieth century, dovetailed bottoms, $335 (pair).

Model home made for 1920s housing development in Cook County, Illinois, $165.

Three drawer hanging box with replaced knobs, walnut, $145.

Freihofer's Quality Cakes display, tin and glass, c. 1915, $350.

Six knives and six forks, c. early 1900s, $95.

Banquet tea server with original stand from a restaurant, c. 1950, stoneware with Albany slip glaze, $175.

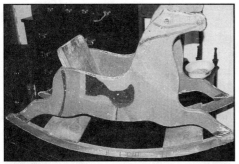

Homemade rocking horse, pine, c. 1920, $275.

Model tool chest for boys, c. 1940, with tools, $85.

Plaster-of-Paris cornucopia, hand painted. c. 1910, $275.

Stoneware jar with "2" stenciled in light cobalt, c. 1890, probably New York state in origin, $55.

Stoneware pitcher and six mugs made for M. J. Dwyer of Bayside, Long Island, dated 1910, $210.

Grocery basket, factory-made, white oak splint, $35.

Homemade doll house, c. 1940-1950, $145.

Oak splint basket with intricately wrapped handle, $65.

Child's wicker rocking chair, c. 1910, $155.

Match stand, c. 1940s, $100.

Match stand from a restaurant, homemade, c. 1940s, $125.

Wooden staved firkin, Golden Drop Plums paper label, gray paint, drop handle, c. 1915, $235.

Set of sleigh bells, c. early 1900s, on original leather strap, $165.

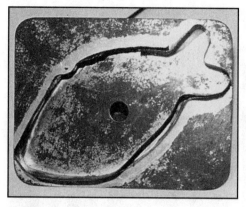

Tin fish cookie cutter, $22.

Tin star cookie cutter, $22.

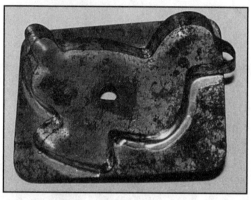

Tin bird cookie cutter, $22.

Tin ax cookie cutter, $26.

Cast iron "bee hive" string holder, c. 1900, $95.

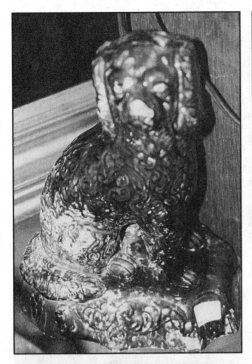

Pine 3-drawer miniature chest with oak graining, c. 1890, $225.

Midwestern molded stoneware dog, rockingham glaze, c. 1880, $125.

Figured maple chest, c. mid-nineteenth century, $1,100.

Twenty-four tube tin candlemold with strap handle, $145.

Art pottery corn mug, c. 1915, $90.

Stoneware chimney toppers, c. late nineteenth century, $135 (each).

Cast iron snow eagle used to hold snow on New England roofs in the late nineteenth century, $95.

Bremner Bros. biscuit tin, $27.

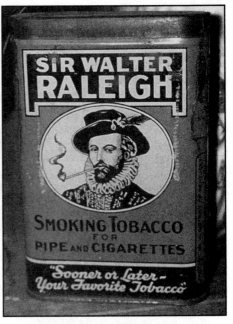

Sir Walter Raleigh pocket tin, $13.

Blue Star Potato Chips tin, c. 1950s, $25.

Sudan Red Pepper tin, $9.

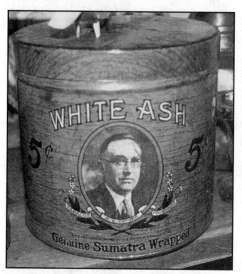

White Ash cigar container, c. 1920s, $9.

Argo Gloss Starch box, $6.

Ginger and ground curry powder tins, $8 (both).

Big Wonder Oil Mop tin, $11.

White Horse Whiskey advertising statue, c. 1940, $75.

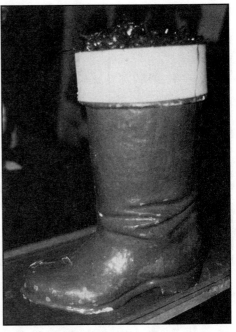

Eight drawer spice chest, factory-made, c. early 1900s, overpainted, $165.

Pressed cardboard Santa boot, c. 1940s, $26.

Cast iron horse watering trough, c. 1890, original red painted surface, $975.

Miniature (5-1/2") candlemold, nineteenth century, 12 tubes, $325.

None Such advertising clock in the form of a pumpkin, working condition, c. 1925, $425.

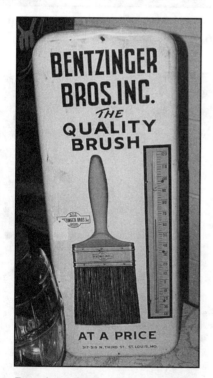

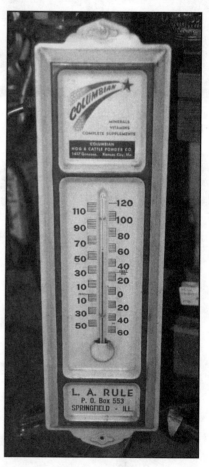

Bentzinger Bros. advertising thermometer, c. 1950s, $55.

L.A. Rule thermometer, c. 1950, $45.

Stoneware Salada Ice Tea container, made for use in a restaurant, c. 1940, $225.

Spindle-back rocking chair, flat seat, original stenciling and decoration, c. 1900, $150.

Collection of 71 pieces of stone fruit, early twentieth century, $5,600.

Wood framed tin sign advertising "Honey for Sale," 5' x 2-1/2', $225.

Philips Choice Vegetable Seeds box, strong interior label, dividers, c. early 1900s, $365.

Shakers Garden Seeds broadside, c. 1860, $1,400.

Five mustard & seed boxes, $2,100.

Five mustard & seed boxes, $2,300.

Stack of five mustard & seed boxes, $4,600.

Six mustard & seed boxes, $3,500.

Rare Shaker Garden
Seeds box, c. 1870,
$2,000.

Eleven seed & mustard boxes, $13,500.

Walnut pie safe with punched star tins, c. 1880, $535.

Oak kitchen cabinet, refinished, c. 1920, $625.

Imported galvanized buckets and containers, $36 (each).

Ovoid stoneware jug with brushed floral decoration, c. 1840, $225.

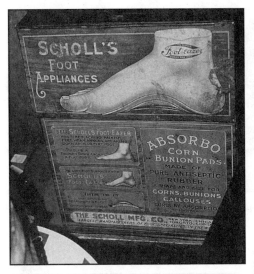

Scholl's Foot Appliances display box, c. 1950, $115.

Painted eye Schoenhut clown, c. 1920s $210.

Schoenhut ringmaster and horse, c. 1920s, $475 (pair).

Schoenhut glass eyed poodle, c. 1920, $485.

Stoneware food mold, c. early twentieth century, $62.

Rockingham food mold, late nineteenth century, $70.

Oval Rockingham soap dish, late nineteenth century, $48.

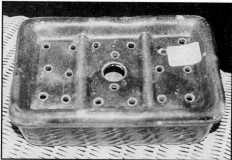

Rectangular Rockingham soap dish, late nineteenth century, $55.

Stoneware vendor's crock marked "John Y. Chisholm 542 Bloomington, IL," c. 1910, $48.

Havana, NY 3 gallon fish crock, slip-trailed decoration, c. 1860, $4,200.

Two gallon stoneware crock with brushed floral decoration, unmarked, c. 1880, $186.

Macomb, IL 15 gallon stoneware crock, stenciled decoration, c. 1900, $115.

Twenty gallon Red Wing storage crock, c. early 1900s, $95.

Fifteen gallon Red Wing storage crock, c. early 1900s, $80.

Stoneware pitcher, 7-1/2" tall, probably Midwestern in origin, c. early 1900s, brushed cobalt bands, $45.

Unusual slip-trailed six gallon butter churn, dated 1870, no maker's mark, $435.

Molded tabletop butter churn with stenciled American Indian logo, c. 1920, $145.

Molded stoneware bedwarmer, c. early 1900s, Bristol glaze, $42.

Stoneware harvest jug, c. 1880, $235.

Belgium resin pots, c. 1940s, $6 (each).

Imported earthenware storage jugs and crocks, $55 (each).

Copper tea kettle, probably English in origin, dovetailed bottom, "drop" handle, nineteenth century, $135.

Log cabin bird house, c. 1940s, $28.

Cast iron dog nutcracker, c. 1920, $125.

Corn sheller, c. 1930, $300.

Corn sheller, c. 1940, $335.

Bowl of wax fruit, c. 1950, $32.

Three late nineteenth century bottles, $27 (all 3).

Enterprise coffee grinder, counter model, paint heavily worn, $300.

Painted galvanized sap buckets, c. 1950, $18 (each).

Galvanized sap buckets, c. 1940s, $14 (each).

Pepsi folding chairs with original blue paint, $45 (each).

Coca-Cola folding chairs from Mexico in original red paint, c. 1960, $55 (each).

Imported French wicker baskets, $40 (each).

Wrought iron boot scraper, probably English in origin, nineteenth century, $96.

Leather doctor's bag, worn but structurally sound, c. early 1900s, $40.

Painted laundry basket, 32" long, $58.

Two copper cooking pots with copper handles, dovetailed bottoms, nineteenth century, $235 (pair).

Concrete windmill weight, shaped like a football, c. 1915, $225.

Cast iron corn bread molds, $55 (each).

Imported watering cans, $35 (each).

County Fair award banner for Grand Champion Bull, 1928, $25.

Six drawer tin spice box with stenciled decoration, c. 1900, $425.

Oak kitchen cabinet with mismatched top, c. early twentieth century, $275.

Glass wine bottle covered with wicker, $20.

Imported wooden "goat" carts, $225 (each).

Twenty-four tube tin candle-mold made into a lamp, $125.

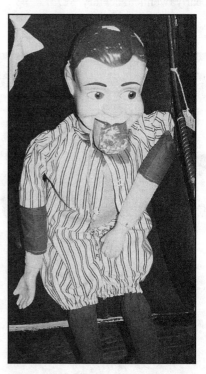

Refinished schoolhouse clock, oak, c. 1910, $250.

Charley McCarthy doll with elongated tongue, c. 1950, $75.

Oversized stone grapes with wooden stem, c. early 1900s, $145.

Sixteen pieces of stone fruit, $640.

Painted pine pie safe, late nineteenth century, $895.

Stripped pine wardrobe, late nineteenth century, $300.

Painted pine blanket chest, dovetailed cast, "as found" condition, $185.

Pepsi-Cola metal chalkboard that listed restaurant specials, c. 1950, $65.

Dome top chest, painted pine, nineteenth century, $145.

1950s seed sacks, $12 (each).

Spice box with interior and exterior labels, early 1900s, $175.

1950s seed sack, $12 (each).

Copper apple butter kettle, dovetailed sides and bottom, southern Illinois in origin, iron "drop" handle, c. 1900, $435.

Plaster-of-Paris vase from Odd Fellows regalia room, c. early 1900s, $35.

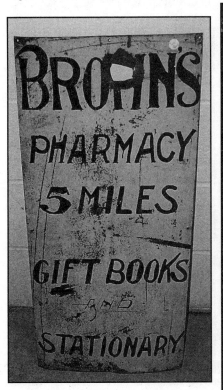

Brown's Pharmacy tin sign, 37" x 16", $135.

Walnut wardrobe, painted white, c. 1890, $900.

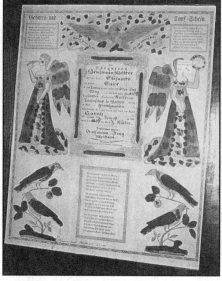

Pennsylvania printed and hand-colored birth certificate, c. 1880, $65.

Felt 3" x 4" flags that were premiums from cigarette packages, c. 1915, $8 (each).

Unusual orange and black painted pine cupboard, $525.

Painted side chair, split-back, c. 1880, $75.

Oversized rye straw basket, 33" diameter, $110.

Three straw filled Santa Claus figures from Germany, c. 1920s, $725 (all three).

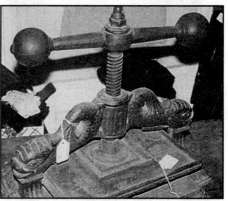

Late nineteenth century cast iron book or cigar mold press, $155.

Nine foot long "Tourist Home" sign, c. 1930s, $285.

Pewter coffee pot, c. 1890s, $225.

Painted pine carpenter's box, c. 1940s, $35.

1940s fireman's helmet, painted red, $55.

Copper wash boiler, $55.

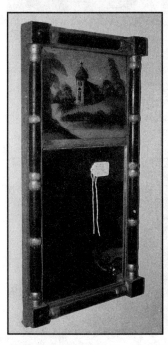

Nineteenth century painted and decorated mirror, $245.

Butler match stand, c. 1940s, $165.

Noisemaker of wood, metal, tin, painted, early 1900s, $145.

California Mid Winter Fair plate, c. 1940s, $45.

Galvanized #6 watering can, $28.

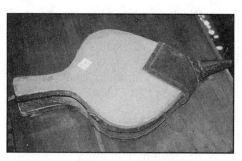

Fireplace bellows, painted red, c. 1900, $65.

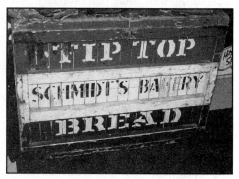

Tip Top Bakery bread storage box, red, white & blue, c. 1930s, $335.

Sign from a less informed time produced by the Lone Star Restaurant Association of Dallas in the 1940s, $95.

Gloss Starch box, c. 1920s, $35.

CHAPTER 4

*H*OT COUNTRY ANTIQUES

Since the late 1970s, there has been a growing interest in sports-related antiques and collectibles. These items range from mounted deer heads to fishing creels and baseball gloves. The interest has been fueled by Ralph Lauren's window displays and print advertisements, country decorating magazines overflowing with the "lodge" look, and a national tendency to seek a more casual and comfortable living style by recapturing something that probably never existed anyway.

Among the many categories of collecting that are receiving increasing interest from collectors are the following:

- Felt pennants with "sewn" on letters
- Fishing reels, lures, and poles
- Fishing creels
- Indiana hickory furniture
- Animal, bird, and fish mounts
- Canoe paddles
- Trophies
- Wool blankets
- Black & white photographs of fishing trips & lodges

- Black & white photographs of local sports teams
- Fishing & hunting related advertising
- College yearbooks and magazines from the 1900-1930 period
- Athletic equipment from 1920-1950
- Baseball memorabilia
- Signs from lodges, fishing camps, and bait shops

Felt Pennants

Felt pennants have been a staple at tourist venues and college bookstores since the late nineteenth century. It was common in the 1890-1940 period to find pennants made of felt with letters and numbers sewn onto the surface celebrating a high school or college.

Dated pennants usually reflect a specific graduating class. In addition to the college and high school pennants, it is not unusual to find fraternities, sorori-

ties, cities, states, and tourist destinations immortalized on felt pennants complete with several nail, tack or moth holes. We have never seen a pennant with "sewn" on letters depicting a professional sports team.

It has been our experience that when a felt pennant shows up at a tag or house sale there are usually multiples rather than a single example somewhere in the immediate vicinity.

Most people didn't stop with one pennant when filling the walls of a bedroom, den, or dormitory room. During both world wars military pennants with American flags celebrating units, campaigns, or training sites were produced in quantity.

We have seen table covers and rugs made from a variety of felt pennants sewn together. Several years ago at the Ramada Inn in Nashville during the Heart of Country week, we saw an oval rug made up of pennants sewn together that was almost 9' in diameter.

Prices for pennants in good condition with "sewn" on letters are, in our view, currently inexpensive compared to where they are going to be in the future.

Niagara Falls pennant with silk American flag, c. 1940s, $85-$100.

Provincetown, MA with unusual lettering resembling logs, c. 1940s, $50-$60.

Green Bay Packers pennant, printed c. 1940s, rarely found in this condition, $150-$175.

High school pennant from Valley High, 1925, $50-$65.

Knox College, Galesburg, IL, pennant c. 1920s, $60-$65.

Adrian College pennant, Michigan, c. 1920, rough condition, possibly homemade, $25-$35.

College pennants from Otterbein, IL, & Heidelberg Otterbein, c. early 1900s, $50-$60; Illinois, c. 1940s, $45-$55; Heidelberg, c. 1940, $50-$55.

Colorado football pennant, c. early 1900s, moth hole, rare with football player, $85-$100.

Martinsville, c. 1930s, probably from Indiana, simple form, $30-$35.

Michigan City (Indiana) pennant, c. 1920s, $30-$35.

C. H. S. pennant, c. 1915, undetermined location, $25-$35.

Yale pillow cover, c. 1940s, $75-$95.

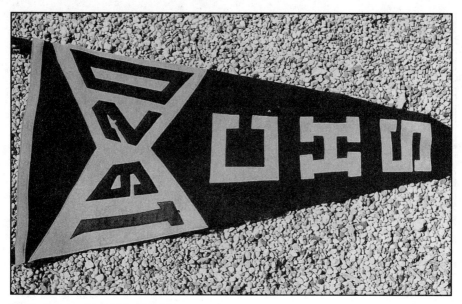

C. H. S. pennant, 1920, $50-$60.

University of Illinois pennant with leather emblem, c. 1940s, $60-$65.

Gem City (Quincy, Illinois) pennant, c. 1930, $30-$35.

Seattle pennant, c. 1920, $30-$35.

Indiana "Shades" pennant, c. 1920, $30-$35.

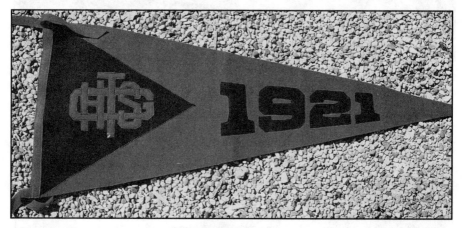

High school pennant, dated 1921, $40-$45.

Illinois pennant, c. 1930s, hand colored emblem, $50-$60.

Maker's names on the back of 1920s pennant.

Close-up of handcolored logo on Illinois pennant.

Later Chicago Pennant Co. tag from about 1940.

Chicago Pennant Co. tag on back of pennant, c. 1920.

Schloss Mfg. Co. of Athens, Ohio, c. 1910, tag on the back of a pennant.

Memphis, Tenn. printed pennant from the 1950s, $15-$18.

Benton Harbor, Michigan printed pennant from the 1950s, $15-$18.

Yale pennant, printed, heavily bleached in color by exposure to the sun, c. 1950s, $5-$8.

Indiana Hickory Furniture

In the past 100 years, there have been at least 10 companies that offered a line of Indiana hickory furniture for sale. The Old Hickory Chair Company of Martinsville, Indiana began in the 1890s and is probably still the most prominent and collectible. There were Indiana hickory furniture companies in Jasper, Vincennes, Terre Haute, Laporte, Colfax, and Martinsville under a variety of ownership. Since 1929, the state farm prison at Putnamville has also been producing hickory furniture.

Over the decades Indiana hickory furniture has been sold for the following:
Vacation homes
Lodges & camps
Motels & hotels
Sanitariums
Health spas
National park lodges
State park cabins, lodges, & offices
Bars
College and public service libraries and buildings

Notes on Collecting Indiana Hickory Furniture

1. Many of the companies did not mark their furniture. A few used paper labels and others, like Old Hickory, branded their wares.
2. Old Hickory furniture can be generally dated by its specific mark.
   a. Old Hickory Chair Company 1890-1921
   b. Old Hickory Furniture Company 1922-1940s
   c. Old Hickory Martinsville, Indiana 1940s-present.
3. Beginning about 1929, Old Hickory put a brass tag on many pieces that indicates the year in which the piece was produced. For example, the two digits "33" on a tag indicate that the piece was made in 1933.
4. Condition is critical to the value of Indiana hickory furniture. If the chair or table has spent time in the weather, the splint or rattan tends to lose any patina. The rest of the piece loses its finish and takes on a greyish cast.
5. The Old Hickory furniture that is being made today is typically as expensive as a comparably made 50 year old example offered for sale at an antiques shop or show.
6. There are dealers who specialize in Indiana hickory furniture and other decorative rustic accessories. The majority advertise regularly in the Maine Antiques Digest.
7. To assume that a significant portion of Indiana hickory stayed in the state is foolish. There were dealers across the country who displayed and sold it. Thousands of pieces were mailed throughout the United States to meet orders.
8. There are legends told about the location of large quantities of Old Hickory furniture placed in storage and forgotten. We have recently heard about a state mental hospital in Indiana that has a huge storeroom filled with pieces that have been damaged or are in need of a new seat or back that have piled up over the years.

We have seen a lodge owned by a corporation in rural Illinois furnished with at least 50 Old Hickory tables, 200 chairs, settees, lamps, and a bar that is used infrequently by employees who have no idea what they are utilizing.

9. The demise of most of the Indiana hickory furniture companies was brought about because of poor management, under capitalization, fires, and changing consumer tastes. The years of the Great Depression put many of the companies so deep in a financial hole that they could never recover.

10. The prices of Indiana hickory will continue to increase because of the following:

   a. the timelessness of the design

   b. the quality of the construction

   c. the difficulty in finding examples to buy

   d. the increasing demand & popularity as more collectors become aware of Indiana hickory furniture and accessories

Old Hickory Price Guide

The 1999 estimated prices are what you could expect to pay at retail at an antiques show or shop from a dealer specializing in Indiana hickory furniture. It is assumed that the pieces of Old Hickory are still in their original condition with minimal signs of misuse.

In about 1920, you could buy the 11 pieces of Old Hickory wholesale for $34.84, if you paid your bill within 30 days of receiving the furniture. The suggested retail price for the 11 pieces was $59.25. The wholesale price does not include shipping charges which would have been relatively minimal 80 years ago.

	Department Store Retail Prices c. 1920	Estimated Antiques Shop Prices c. 2000
#24 chair	$2.75	$175-$225
#25 rocker	$3.50	$275-$350
#110 settee	$5.50	$600-$775
#32 chair	$4.00	$400-$500
#33 rocker	$4.75	$425-$525
#104 settee	$11.00	$1,600-$2,000
#225 table	$5.00	$300-$350
#38 chair	$3.50	$300-$375
#39 rocker	$4.25	$300-$375
#138 settee	$7.50	$1,200-$1,550
#238 swing & chains	$7.50	$600-$750

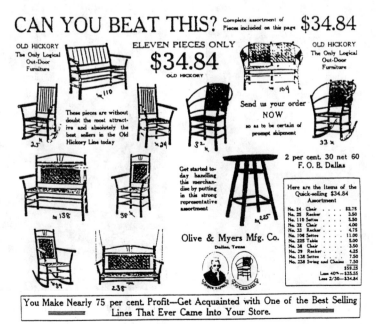

Old Hickory rocking chair with rattan, $475-$575.

Old Hickory side chair with splint, $275-$350.

1930s Old Hickory side chair with rattan, $330.

Old Hickory arm chair with rattan, $350-$400.

Old Hickory rocking chair with splint seat, $400.

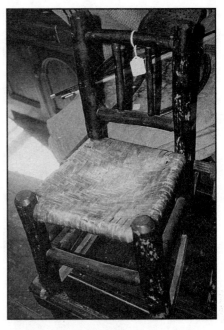

Hickory child's chair with splint seat, maker unknown, $85.

Unmarked Indiana hickory rocking chair with splint seat, c. 1940, $275.

Equestrian coat and pair of riding boots, $250 (coat and boots).

Pair of early 1900s snow shoes from Wisconsin, $275.

Pair of 1930s snow shoes, $225.

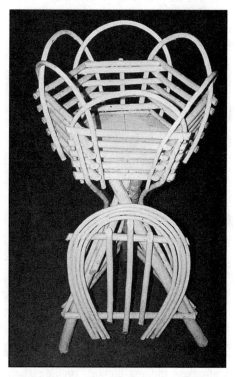

Rustic tobacco stand, found in Wisconsin, c. 1940s, $185.

Rustic plant stand, painted white, $75.

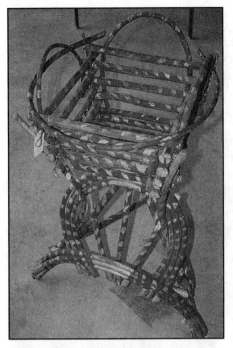

Rustic plant stand painted green with white spots, c. 1930s, $95.

Blue painted stand or bedside table, c. early 1900s, $135-$150.

Wooden tennis rackets from the 1920s, $15 (each).

1950s tennis rackets, wooden, $20 (each).

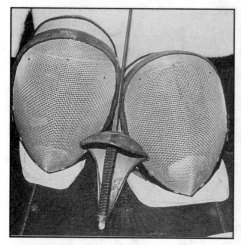

Fencing masks, $24 (each).

Die-cut Beacon Blanket sign, almost life-size, c. 1930, $2,200-$2,500.

1930s fishing creel with leather trim and fishing net; creel, $165; net, $35.

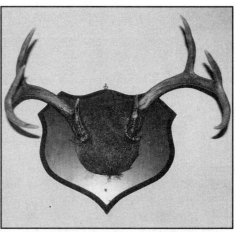

Mounted deer horns, $5.

Deer mount, probably dates from the 1950s, $150.

Squirrel mount, logs, and nuts, c. 1950, $65.

Fish decorated serving plate, c. 1915, $55.

Joos Kennels sign, c. 1940s-tin frame and sign, 40" x 38", $400-$500.

Plaster-of-Paris Indian chief lamp, c. 1940s, $95.

Plaster-of-Paris Indian brave and maiden lamp, c. 1950, $135.

Locker room door used by future Hall of Famer Greg Maddux while playing for the Peoria (IL) Chiefs, $250.

Game-used Mike Schmidt bat, Louisville Slugger, $600.

Bat autographed by 17 members of the Baseball Hall of Fame, $395.

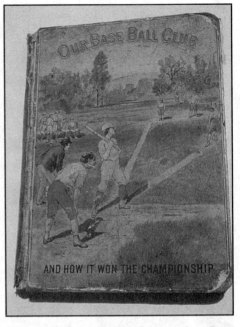

Game used batting gloves of Giant's infielder Chili Salowitz, c. 1994, $30 (pair).

First book of baseball fiction, *Our Base Ball Club & How It Won The Championship*, 1884, $175.

Wrigley Field wooden seat, $275.

Rare orange painted seat from Crosley Field, $500.

University of Illinois athletic sweater, 1907, $300.

Cereal premium hat with Babe Ruth stitched signature, 1930s, $250.

Babe Ruth Underwear box, c. 1920s, $400.

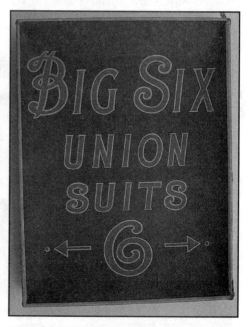

Big Six Union Suits box, c. 1915, "Big Six" was New York Giants' pitcher Christy Mathewson, $60.

Die-cut Moxie advertisement with Ted Williams, 1950s, $750.

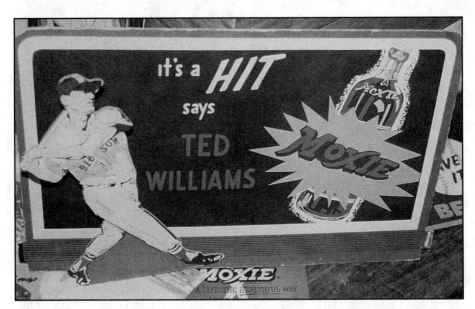

Three-dimensional Ted Williams Moxie counter display, c. 1960, $750.

Six pack of Ted Williams' Root Beer, c. 1950s, $500.

Adhesive sticker for Ted's Root Beer, $15.

Official League Ball radio in working order, 1940s, $800.

Baseball autographed by John Mize, Hank Aaron, & Stan Musial, $100.

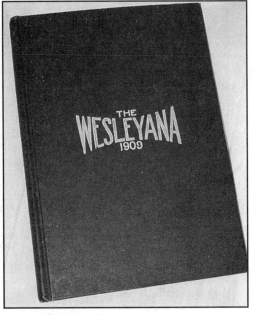

1909 Wesleyana yearbook, Illinois Wesleyan University, Bloomington, Illinois, $30.

1958 Willie Mays Hartland statue, $425.

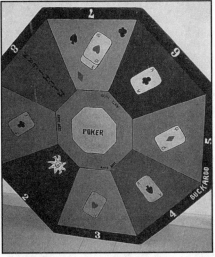

Poker table top of Baseball Hall of Fame member Ed Roush purchased at his estate sale in Oakland City, Indiana, $300.

1958 Ted Williams and Yogi Berra Hartland statues, Williams $450; Berra $400.

1910 Reach American League Base Ball Guide, $75.

1916 Spalding's Baseball Guide, $75.

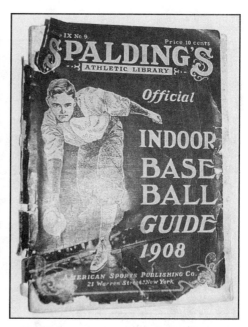

1908 Spalding's Indoor Base Ball Guide, $15.

1889 Spalding Base Ball Guide, $200.

Pinch Hit paper broadside, 42" long x 26", c. 1930s, $325.

Rug made from felt pennants with sewn-on letters, c. 1920, 4' x 3', made up of colleges, $275.

Basketball signed by former UCLA coach John Wooden, $175.

Basketball signed by Julius Irving, $200.

Murray State University football game helmet, $200.

1950 football helmet and shoulder pads, $50 (set).

Brown and Bigelow 1952 Connie Mack calendar in Hall of Fame series, $300.

Brown and Bigelow 1957 Joe DiMaggio calendar, $325.

1953 Brown and Bigelow John McGraw calendar, $250.

1967 Brown and Bigelow Christy Mathewson calendar, $350.

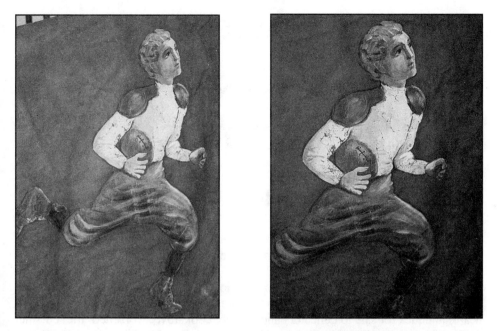

1908 leather pennant used by Ill. State Normal University to lead football team onto the field, $400.

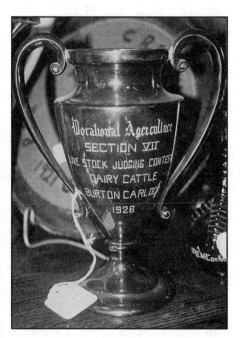

1928 live-stock judging trophy, $40.

High school basketball trophy from 1930, $135.

CHAPTER 5
KITCHEN AND HEARTH ANTIQUES

Stoneware Price Guide

This chapter was prepared by Teri and Joe Dziadul. It illustrates items from their personal collection. The Dziaduls have been filling special requests for more than 25 years and offer kitchen and hearth antiques for sale to collectors and dealers. The current list of items for sale may be obtained by sending $2 to the Dziaduls at 6 S. George Washington Road, Enfield, CT 06082.

Early diarists in New England provide us with interesting details that document the kitchen's appearance in the 18th and 19th centuries. To establish a new household, some basic items included cast-iron kettles, trivets, toasters, trammels and hooks for hearth cooking. Spits and roasting jacks were essential accessories. A peel and bread baking pans were necessary for the beehive bake ovens.

Pies, cakes and breads were baked in a Dutch oven between baking days. It stood on three legs over the coals and was fitted with a deep lid onto which glowing coals were heaped to provide even heat above and below. For the most part, New England dinners came out of heavy black iron pots. The New England boiled dinner was triumphant over the limitations of fireplace cookery. It simmered for hours without attention. A tin kitchen stood in the hearth and turned out pies, cakes, and roasts.

About 1850, the old fireplaces were closed up and the new source of heat was the cast-iron stove. Many believed the cookstove worsened the cuisine. Harriet Beecher Stowe expressed this sentiment when she wrote that, "...an open fireplace is an altar of patriotism. Would our Revolutionary fathers have gone barefooted and bleeding over snows to defend airtight stoves and cooking ranges? I trow not. It was the memory of this great open kitchen fire...lits roaring, hilarious voice of invitation, its dancing tongues of flame, that called to them through the snows of that dreadful winter...."

Twenty years later, the Yankee kitchen displayed many marvels. The heavy iron pots were replaced with lighter ware. Firing up the cook stove, the housewife could make toast, boil the coffee and coddle eggs.

The yearnings for the nostalgic age of homespun account for the passion collectors crave in kitchen and hearth collectibles. The warmth of simple country life can be enjoyed in a city apartment as well as a country retreat or home. The dwindling number of scarce examples is causing prices to advance dramatically.

Spot the trends and look for categories with potential investment growth. For the most part, look for quality. A fine example is a better choice when making a decision to buy rather than several inferior ones. Acquire the best of the past for future enrichment.

Tin nutmeg grater, $850-$1,000; apple parer, $375-$475.

Beveled edge, 1-quart Dazey churn, c. 1906-1912, $1,200-$2,000; John Jones patent, Oct. 23, 1900, 1/2-gallon beater, $1,500-$1,800.

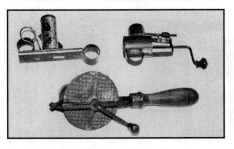

One hand patent applied for nutmeg grater, $350-$450; Pat. Sept. 4, 1877 nutmeg grater, $650-$850; pat. Jan. 30, 1877 wood handle nutmeg grater, $650-$850.

Monroe one minute egg timer, $2,000-$3,000.

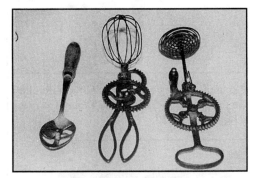

Propeller spoon, $400-$500; Jaquette Bros. scissors beater, $850-$1,200; P.D. & Co. beater, $1,300-$1,500.

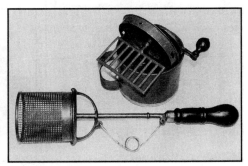

Uriah D. Seltzer's Lebanon Beater, c. 1892, $475-$600; Perfection, pat. May 13, '84 beater, $350-$450.

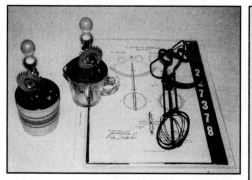

A & J pat. blue banded beater jar, $125-$150; A & J beater jar, $125-$150.

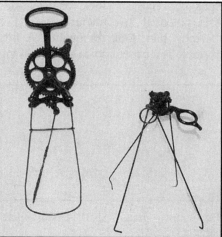

Morse and L. Burnham beater, $1,500-$2,000.

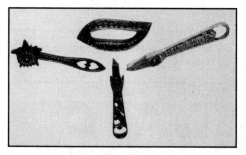

Patented can openers, $45-$65; Cinderella pie crimper, $85-$125; C.D. Kenny Co. pot scraper, $75-$125.

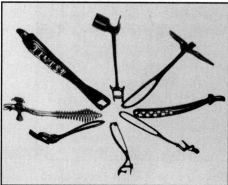

Stove lid lifters, $50-$75.

Corrugated rollers washboard, $150-$200; NuWash washboard, $200-$300.

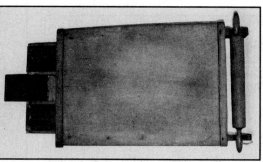

Combination pastry board, rolling pin, and drawers for flour, sugar, and baking powder. Piece has personal inscription and 1874 date, $600-$700.

Grand Union Tea Company coffee grinder, made by Griswold, $500-$600.

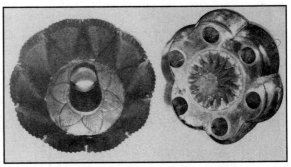

Preserve jars, circa 1890 with ribbing on outside of lid, $25-$40; stack of jelly glasses with tin lids, $15-$35; Flaccus currant jelly jar, $90-$130.

Decorative tin cake pans, $150-$175.

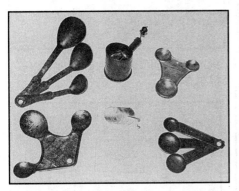

Miniature Hunter flour sifter, $525-$575; advertising measuring spoons, $65-$85.

Chagrin Falls, O. iron, $125-$150; lady on liberty dollar iron, $75-$100; gem iron, $75-$100; Sensible #6 iron, $150-$175.

Rectangular fancy wire bakery display tray, $250-$295.

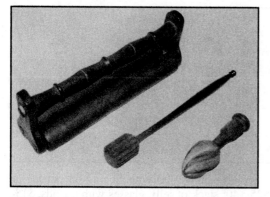

Wood double rolling pin, $500-$600; muddler, $75-$85; lemon reamer, unusual head, $175-$225.

Non-pariel apple parer, $900-$1,000; Champion apple parer, $1,400-$1,600.

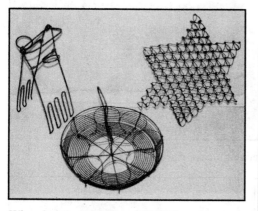

Wire helping hands, $75-$95; wire egg holder, $80-$125; star trivet, $70-$85.

North's patent cast-iron griddle 7-19-87, $225-$275.

Preserve jars with labels, depending on condition of jar and label, $500-$800; pat. 1869 apple segmenter, $700-$900.

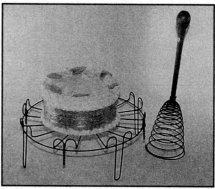

Round wire cake stand, $85-$95; spiral wire beater, $35-$45.

Bryant and May nutmeg grater box, $375-$475; Cerosta match holder, $225-$295.

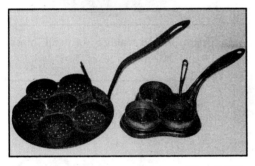

Cast iron and tin egg poacher, pat. Nov. 3 '85, $95-$125; silvers, Brooklyn tin pat. egg poacher, $75-$95.

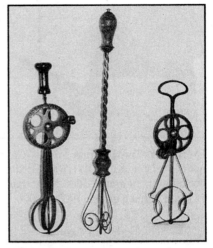

Advertising beater, "Use Minard's Liniment-King of Pain", $1,200-$1,800; Ashley beater, $1,200-$1,400; brown patent beater, $1,200-$1,500.

All wood flour sifter, $295-$395.

Golfer door stop, $675-$775.

EverReady, Turner Brass Works, Chicago, Ill. nutmeg grater, $1,500-$1,800; Bilston enamel pocket nutmeg grater, $600-$800; pat. Feb. 27, 1877 tin nutmeg grater, $900-$1,000.

Brown Bread baking tin with brass plaque, $65-$75.

Patented device for churning, $1,300-$1,500.

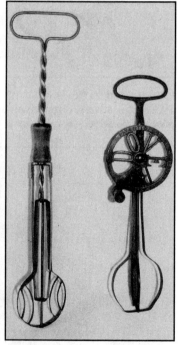

Oval bakery display tray, $225-$275; rectangular bakery display tray, $150-$195; rolling pin, perpendicular handle, $425-$495; cutting board with sides, $125-$175; double ended cookie and doughnut cutter, $65-$75; combination cookie and doughnut cutter, $25-$35.

Thomas W. Brown patent Archimaedes egg beater, the Clipper model, $350-$400; Dover cast in the gear wheel beater, $275-$375.

Stacking jars for Nabisco Crackers, $185-$250.

Painted tin canister, $200-$250.

Tin candle box, $295-$395.

Iron cannonball muffin pan, $175-$195.

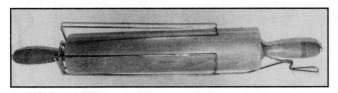

Rolling pin with tin wire holder, rolling pin is marked Thorpe Rolling Pin Co, Cheshire, Conn, $175-$195.

Multiple cookie cutters in oval frame: Christmas cutters (at right), $450-$550; cutters, $275-$300.

Crystal coffee bean grinder, $125-$195.

Miniatures: chopping board, $35-$45; cake tin, $30-$35; spice tower, $250-$295; butter pat dish, $150-$195.

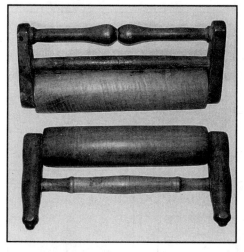

Framed wooden rolling pins, $375-$475.

Wooden nutmeg grater, $775-$975; miniature spice tower, $350-$450; oval storage boxes with labels, $300-$350 each.

Storage jar with tin lid on marked wire trivet base, $125-$150.

Large tin flour sifter marked NASH, $75-$85.

Sargent Foster apple parer mounted on board for sitting accommodation, $125-$160.

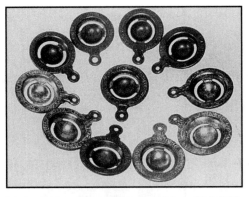

Tin egg separators with advertising, $20-$75.

Peaseware egg cups on stand, $1,500-$2,000.

Oval wire bakery display tray, rare form, $225-$275.

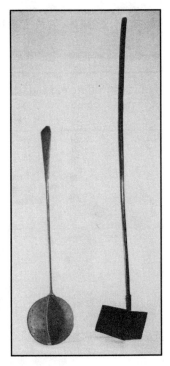

Milliners head model, $1,500-$2,000; wooden glove forms, $350-$400.

United Banana Split ice-cream scoop, $625-$695.

Tin and iron tallow skimmer, $375-$450; ember carrier, $350-$450.

Half round or demilune butter stamp, $600-$800; gray pottery butter crock with blue banding, $150-$175.

Springerle rolling pin and boards: rolling pin, $375-$475; boards, $175-$275.

Tin beeswax cake mold for seamstress use, $195-$225.

Batter jug with tin covers, $225-$275.

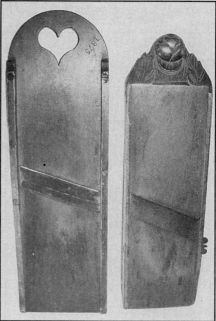

Slaw cutting boards: dated 1875, heart cut-out hanger, $275-$375; carved cabbage rose and leaves, $325-$400.

Large chopping or cutting board with sides, $125-$175; miniature tea service with butterfly handles, $175-$195; single brass candlestick, $75-$85.

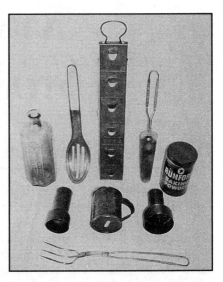

Yellowware bowl and custard cups: bowl with blue bands, $85-$100; cups with blue bands, $40-$50.

Rumford collectibles: glass Rumford bottle, $45-$65; mixing spoon, $24-$28; potato baker, $75-$95; spatula, $18-$24; can, $20-$25; biscuit cutter, $15-$20; measuring cup, $35-$45; doughnut cutter, $15-$20; fork, $18-$24.

Milk glass lemon squeezer embossed Sunkist, $40-$50.

Matched yellowware set of custard cups and mixing bowl, blue banding on yellow ground, $175-$195.

Many thanks to:
Lois Carey, J. Delphia, B & D Allen, Donna Krebs, Helen Storey, J & D Hoy, G & E Clark, P. Seidel, K. Playfair, I. & R. Arnold, J & P Moffet, B & K Grossman, T & P Manfredi, J & B Butt, Carol Bohn, D & S Ryan, D. DeMore, N. Kosiewski, John Lambert, D. Perry, B. Crane, R & B Ulmer who shared their collections at a recent convention of Kollectors of Old Kitchenware.

CHAPTER 6

STONEWARE

Decorated Stoneware

It is possible to pay $50 or $2,500 for a jug or crock made from identical clay, thrown at the same potter's wheel, produced on the same day, fired in the same kiln, and sold from the same vendor's cart. The only difference in the value of the two pieces of stoneware is the quality of the cobalt decoration each carries.

A two gal. crock from Lyons, New York with a slip-trailed swipe of cobalt across its front has 50 times less value than a similar example with a slip-trailed deer surrounded by trees and leaves. A deer crock is also considered a rare piece of American folk art that is eagerly sought after by collectors. When it is objectively evaluated, we find a $50 piece of stoneware decorated with a $2,450 cobalt deer. The $2,500 deer crock can have some serious structural problems and still maintain much of its value if it is professionally restored.

Another type of crock is one holding two gals. and bearing a swipe of cobalt. This is considered an excellent candidate to be a doorstop filled with magazines. However, in this case, if the $50 crock has a crack, its value is even more minimal.

Collecting Decorated Stoneware

Any collector has to realize that stoneware in nineteenth century America was utilitarian. It was purchased inexpensively, treated with little respect, and disposed of when severely cracked, chipped, or broken. Used for storage and pickling, it was commonly available in most areas of the East and Midwest at local potteries.

A piece of stoneware offered for sale today is sometimes described in auction catalogs or advertisements as having "drying lines," "hairlines," or "through" cracks. A "drying line" is primarily a cosmetic problem that developed while the piece was being dried before it was placed in the kiln for firing.

A "hairline" crack is exactly what its name implies. It is a thin break or crack in the surface of the stoneware that does not go all the way through the piece. The problem with the "hairline" is that it has the potential at some point to work its way completely through the piece and become a serious problem unless it is repaired.

Once a crack is "through" it must be professionally restored if the piece is going to be kept intact. The "through" crack is not a death sentence for a piece of stoneware but it usually leaves it in critical condition.

Occasionally a piece of stoneware appears to have a blurred or out of focus cobalt decoration. This is usually caused by the kiln being too hot during the firing process combined with too much water in the cobalt slip. The mixture of cobalt oxide and slip (liquid clay) burns or bubbles away. Excessive heat can also turn the blue cobalt black.

If the proximity of the piece of stoneware is too close to the fire in the kiln, the glaze can be burned away or brown spots can appear. The greenish bubbles that sometimes are on the surface of a crock or jug are called "salt tears." They normally do not have negative affects on the value of a piece, unless they interfere with cobalt decoration. Salt tears are caused when the kiln cools rapidly with too much salt in it.

Decoration

To some extent it is possible to date a piece of stoneware by its form or shape and the manner in which it was decorated. From the late eighteenth century until the 1830s, most American stoneware was ovoid or pear-shaped in form and the pieces that were decorated contained flowers or patriotic scenes executed with a metal tool or a sharp wire. This scratching process is more scholarly known as incising.

As the demand for stoneware brought about an increase in the number of potteries and competition for business, the incising method of decoration became too labor intensive and gradually gave way to slip-cupping or trailing.

Slip-trailing involved pouring a thin line of cobalt slip from a cup that left a raised line of cobalt on the surface of the piece. This process was popular from the 1830s until the 1880s. The most detailed slip-trailing took place in the 1850s and 1860s.

Brushes dipped in cobalt slip were used for decorating stoneware between the 1850s and the 1880s. The most elaborate pieces usually date from the 1860s through the late 1870s, but there are some spectacular examples that were produced by special order into the early 1900s.

The evolution from incising to slip-trailing to brush painting was caused by the constant demand to speed up the process and meet the increasing competition and mass production of stoneware utilitarian household pieces. From the 1880s through the first quarter of the twentieth century, the technique of choice at most potteries was stenciling. It saved even more time and cut even deeper into labor costs. At this point, most collectors of nineteenth century decorated stoneware pay little attention to stenciled examples. However, eventually they are going to become more attractive as supplies of brush, incised, and slip-trailed pieces evaporate.

Cobalt Decorated Stoneware

One gal. ovoid crock from South Amboy, New Jersey that dates from about 1805. This piece has impressed and tooled decoration around the rim of the piece and incised and cobalt accented double scallops on the front. Pieces this early are rare.

The four gal. slightly ovoid crock was slip-trailed with cobalt double flowers about 1865.

This rare five gal. cake crock was made at the West Troy, New York Pottery about 1880.

This three gal. jug was a product of J. & E. Norton Pottery of Bennington, Vermont about 1859. The detailed peacock on a stump with ground cover is highly detailed and rare.

The six gal. crock was probably a special order piece from H. M. Whitson of Havana, New York about 1861. The detail of the cobalt slip is rare.

T. Harrington, Lyons, New York butter churn with a detailed running fox that has been slip-trailed. It dates from about 1855.

Brushed flower crock from P. Mugler of Buffalo, New York from the middle of the nineteenth century and a slip-trailed flower from C. W. Braun of Buffalo. The Braun piece has a slip-trailed two gal. capacity mark and dates from about 1870.

Stoneware at Auction

Bruce and Vicki Waasdorp have conducted spring and fall decorated stoneware auctions by mail and telephone for almost a decade. Prior to each auction, they have a fully illustrated catalog for collectors to study. Each piece of stoneware offered for sale in the auction is pictured and described in detail. The quality of the photographs and the use of selected items in color add a great deal to the collector's ability to view the pieces. Collectors may use the telephone, mail, or fax to place and raise their bids within a specific time frame. Following the auction each subscriber to the catalog receives a prices-realized listing.

We have found the Waasddorp's auction catalogs to be an outstanding price guide for monitoring trends among stoneware collectors.

For more information about future stoneware auctions, contact:

Bruce & Vicki Waasdorp
P.O. Box 434, 10931 Main Street
Clarence, NY 14031
(716) 759-2361 (telephone)
(716) 759-2397 (fax)
http://www.antiques-stoneware.com

The following pieces of stoneware were sold through the Waasdorp decorated stoneware auction on October 4, 1998. The prices include the 10% buyer's premium.

Approximate 1 gal. unsigned crock with brush blue swan design, attributed to Pottery Works, Little West 12th St. N.Y., c. 1870, $1,045; Unsigned 2 gal. crock, probably Cortland, N.Y., boldly decorated with an unusual flower, short horizontal through line at the base on the side and 2 rim chips, 9-1/2" tall, c. 1870, $132.

Unsigned 3 gal. pitcher with blue accents, unusual size for this form of pottery, large glued freeze cracks emanating from the base all around, 15-1/2" tall, c. 1850, $165; Edmands & Co. three gal. jug with carved wooden stopper, thick blue leaf and vine design top to bottom, stone ping and long glaze spider lines on the side, kiln burn on the front in the making, 15" tall, c. 1870, $220.

Edmands & Co. 2 gal. jar with simple slip flower design, 12-1/2" tall, c. 1870, $198; Edmands & Co. 4 gal. jar with stylized slip leaf design, glued rim chip on the front and minor stone ping on the left side, 15" tall, c. 1870, $110.

E. Selby & Co., Hudson, N.Y., 2 gal. jug with ribbed and dotted flower decoration, uncommon maker's mark, 13-1/2" tall, c. 1850; Albany, N.Y., approximate 2 gal. jar with thick blue bird design, replacement stoneware lid, excellent condition, 11-1/2" tall, c. 1860, $220.

I. Seymour, Troy, N.Y., 1 gal. jug with blue accents, tight through lines at the shoulder, glaze spider and overall staining, 11-1/2" tall, c. 1850, $44; West Troy, N.Y., 5 gal. cake crock with large standing dog, rare form & design, short tight line on the back and a few minor interior surface chips, 13" diameter, c. 1880, $2,750.

Unsigned 6 liter ovoid crock with applied open handles, decorated front and back in rare ochre (dark brown color), probably German origin, rare & early piece, 9-1/2" tall, c. 1810, $220; Approximate 1 gal. ovoid jug with rare dark brown ochre flower, unglazed stack marks in the making, 11" tall, c. 1830, $880.

L. Seymour, Troy, N.Y., factory piece, approx. 4 gal., uncommon double handles, ovoid, blue brush tree, professional restoration to freeze cracks up from the base in front, early maker's mark, 18" tall, c. 1810, $716; unsigned 4 gal. ovoid jug, large incised leaf design, very early, probably New York City origin, some staining and a few surface chips from use, 17" tall, c. 1820, $577.50.

Unsigned 3 gal. ovoid bowl with brush plume repeated front and back, professional restoration to age cracks throughout, some interior lime staining, attributed to Hudson Valley region of N.Y., 11" tall, c. 1840, $275; unsigned 2 gal. ovoid crock with deeply incised blue accent flower, very early, probably New York City origin, 10" tall, c. 1790, $385.

Unsigned 2 gal. ovoid jug with incised and blue accented cluster of cherries, rare New York City origin, 13-1/2" tall, c. 1820, $880; P. Cross, Hartford, 2 gal. ovoid jug with incised and blued flower, extremely rare mark, professional restoration to age lines, surface chips at the spout, 16" tall, c. 1805, $990.

S. Amboy, New Jersey, 1 gal. ovoid crock with applied and open handles, impressed and tooled decoration around the rim & incised and blue double scalloped design in the front, 5" almost invisible through line in the front, 9-1/2" tall, c. 1805, $2,530; J. Remmey, Manhattan Wells, New York, 1 gal. ovoid crock, free of any damage but misshapen in the making, almost 9" tall, c. 1795, $3,410.

I. Seymour, Troy, N.Y., 2 gal. ovoid jug with incised and blue filled bird, 13-1/2" tall, c. 1825, $1,705; I. Seymour & Co. Troy, N.Y., approximate 2 gal. ovoid jug with blue accent at name and incised leaf and flower decor, professional restoration to stone ping on side, otherwise excellent, 14" tall, c. 1827, $605.

Norton & Fenton, Bennington, V.T., 2 gal. ovoid jug with brushed triple flower, glued chip at the spout and some clay discoloration from the making, 12-1/2" tall, c. 1845, $385; D. Roberts & Co. Utica, approximate 2 gal. ovoid jug with brush decoration, overall staining and glaze spiders at the spout, 12" tall, c. 1828, $330.

N. White, Utica, N.Y., 2 gal. ovoid jug with brushed flower, dark blue decoration, glaze burn and stack marks in the making, 13" tall, c. 1840, $275; N. White, Utica, N.Y., 1 gal. ovoid jar with lid, "1" surrounded with blue accents at name and handles, surface chipping all around the rim, 1" tight line on the front, 9" tall, c. 1850, $209.

S. Blair, Cortland, N.Y., 2 gal. ovoid jug, faint blue brushed flower, 13" tall, c. 1830, $176; I. Seymour, Troy, N.Y., 2 gal. ovoid jug with brushed flowers, professional restoration to chips at handle & spout, tight line extending to the base in the front but not in the blue, 13-1/2" tall, c. 1825, $121.

N. Clark & Co. Mt. Morris, 3 gal. ovoid crock with brushed "3," uncommon maker, 12-1/2" tall, c. 1840, $302.50; S. S. Perry & Co., West Troy, N.Y., 1 gal. jug with brushed accent at the name, 10-1/2" tall, c. 1833, $302.50.

S. Hart 1 gal. ovoid jug, simple brush design, hole on one side from a stone ping and a deep thumb impression on the back, 10" tall, c. 1840, $165; H. & G. Nash, Utica, N.Y., 1 gal. jug with brushed flower design, incised very deeply with double snake design, extremely rare, minor glaze spider on the back, 11" tall, c. 1835, $1,100.

J. F. Brayton & Co., Utica, N.Y., 1 gal. ovoid jar with delicate brushed flower, 5" through line up from the base in the front, 9" tall, c. 1830, $132; Chollar Darby & Co., Cortland, N.Y., 1 gal. ovoid crock with brushed blue decor, glued x-shaped long lines on the back, 9" tall, c. 1840, $110.

J. Fisher, Lyons, N.Y., 1 gal. vendor's jug, 10-1/2" tall, c. 1880, $132; Cooperative Pottery, Lyons, N.Y., 1 gal. advertising jug, 6" j-shaped line in front extending from the base, tight line in the handle, 11" tall, c. 1880, $187.

Unsigned 1 gal. jug impressed and blue accented "Fuchhs Bro's Importers of Wines, Liquors, Cigars ETC 510 Main St. Buffalo, N.Y.," 13" tall, c. 1860, $77; unsigned and undecorated 1 gal. advertising jug, "H.F. Reynolds Manufacturer of Linseed Oil, White Lead and Zinc in Oil, Sash, Doors, and Blinds, 9 Buffalo St." 13" tall, c. 1850, $99.

Haxstun & Co., Ft. Edward, N.Y., 3 gal. jug "Cushman & Co. Importers of Wines," 15-1/2" tall, c. 1880, $385; J. Fisher, Lyons, N.Y., 2 gal. jug, professional restoration to chips at handle, 13" tall, c. 1880, $132.

W. A. Macquoid & Co. Pottery Works, Little West 12th St. N.Y., 3 gal. jar, uncommon cherries design, age spiders on the very back, 14" tall, c. 1870, $1,375; unsigned 1 gal. handled pouring pitcher with three roses, definitely produced by W. A. Macquoid & Co. Pottery Works, Little West 12th St., N.Y., 11" tall, c. 1870, $2,530.

W. A. Macquoid & Co. Pottery Works, Little West 12th St. N.Y., 5 gal crock with rare cluster of grapes, 4" hairline at the ear on the right side, 12" tall, c. 1865, $1,320.

Unsigned 1 gal. crock with duck in pond design, attributed to Macquoid & Co. N.Y., excellent condition, 7" tall, c. 1860, $1,155; unsigned 2 gal. jug with fruit design, possibly Macquoid Pottery, 13-1/2" tall, c. 1870, $275.

S. Hart, Fulton, N.Y., 4 gal. crock with double birds, very tight 7" through line in front, 7" tight through on the side, up from the base, 11" tall, c. 1875, $522.50; J. Darrow & Sons, Baldwinsville, N.Y., 2 gal. ovoid crock, thick blue flower, minor design fry & restoration to glaze flake spots on the side, uncommon mark, 10" tall, c. 1876, $198.

S. Hart, Fulton, N.Y., 3 gal. crock with thick blue bird, glaze spider on the very back, 10-1/2" tall, c. 1877, $577.50; S. Hart, Fulton, N.Y., with crossed lovebirds, y-shaped through line bottom and extending 6" up the back, lime staining and a stone ping on the front, 9-1/2" tall, c. 1875, $357.50.

Reidinger & Caire, Poughkeepsie, N.Y., 3 gal. jug with brushed double flower, half dollar size surface chip at the base on the side, 14" tall, c. 1870, $143; Reidinger & Caire, 5 gal. crock with a large bird on a plume, excellent condition, 12" tall, c. 1870, $907.50.

Unsigned 2 gal. crock with bird on a branch, probably Ellenville, N.Y., very minor through line at the base on the side, 9" tall, c. 1880, $220; unsigned 2 gal. crock with light blue chicken pecking corn design, probably Ellenville, N.Y., chips at the rim interior, 9-1/2" tall, c. 1885, $302.50.

Roberts, Binghamton, N.Y., 5 gal. crock with large bird on triple flower design, base chip in the front and a few glaze flake spots, 13-1/2" tall, c. 1860, $550; unsigned 4 gal. advertising jar with lid, decorated with a large dotted bird landing on a flower, professional restoration to 2 tight lines extending from the rim, 15-1/2" tall, c. 1860, $797.50.

Jordan, 1 gal. jug with thick blue male profile surrounded by a vine, extremely rare design, restoration to handle, 12" tall, c. 1850, $1,320; J. M. Burney & Son, Jordan, 4 gal. ovoid crock with unusual bird, 11" long on 8" leafy branch, 8" glued y-shaped crack on the back, peppered finish to the glaze in the making, 13-1/2" tall, c. 1855, $3,740.

Jordan, approximately 1-1/2 gal. ovoid crock with brushed blue leaf design, large stack mark on the side & overall staining, 8-1/2" tall, c. 1850, $143; Jordan, 1 gal. ovoid jug with brushed blue design, excellent condition, 10" tall, c. 1850, $247.50.

A. O. Wittemore, Havana, N.Y., 6 gal. butter churn with double flower, 10" through line on back extending from the rim and a 3" line at the right ear, 18" tall, c. 1870, $990; H. M. Whitman, Havana, N.Y., 6 gal. crock with large vine & double grapes, kiln burn in the front and a long j-shaped line on the back, 13-1/2" tall, c. 1861, $2,750.

T. Harrington, Lyons, N.Y., 2 gal. ovoid jug with light blue brushed plume design, 15" tall, c. 1865, $187; T. Harrington, 3 gal. cream pot, starface design, two 5" tight through lines on either side of the design, 12" tall, c. 1860, $3,520.

T. Harrington, 2 gal. preserve jar with lid, wreath design, 11-1/2" tall, c. 1860, $632.50; T. Harrington, 2 gal. preserve jar with brushed plume, some discoloration & minor age spiders on the sides & back, 3 very tight through lines extending from the rim, 11-1/2" tall, c. 1860, $132.

J. Fisher, Lyons, N.Y., 2 gal. jug with bold snow flake design, few minor glaze flakes and a large surface chip in the handle, 13" tall, c. 1880, $275; J. Fisher, 2 gal. jug with "Lyons" in blue script, surface chip at the spout, 13-1/2" tall, c. 1880, $715.

Lyons, 2 gal. jar with brushed blue flower, surface chips at the rim and some overall staining & glaze spiders, 11" tall, c. 1880, $198; Lyons, 2 gal. jug with brushed flower, excellent condition, 1-1/2" tall, c. 1870, $257.50.

Lyons, 2 gal. jar with dark blue flower, minor signs of stack marks, professional restoration to spout chip, 13-1/2" tall, c. 1866, $143; Lyons, 2 gal. ovoid crock with brushed blue double flower, large stone ping, on the side, 4" very tight line in front, some surface wear, 10" tall, c. 1860, $165.

J. Fisher, Lyons, N.Y., 6 gal. crock with large blue double flower, full length glued crack in the front, through the design, 14" tall, c. 1880, $132; J. Fisher & Co., 4 gal. crock with thick blue hops design, excellent condition, 11-1/2" tall, c. 1880, $440.

John Burger, Rochester, 2 gal. jug with signature sunflower design, 8" very tight spider on the side, 13-1/2" tall, c. 1865, $907.50; N. Clark, Rochester, 2 gal. jar with bold cabbage style flower, includes the lid, professional restoration to rim chip in front & a tight line on the back, 12" tall, c. 1850, $797.50.

John Burger, Rochester, N.Y., 2 gal. jar with lid, slip decorated flower design, 11" tall, c. 1865, $467.50; John Burger, Rochester, 2 gal. pail shaped crock with large blue flower, very short undetectable hairline on the back, 9" tall, c. 1854, $330.

Burger Brothers, Rochester, 2 gal. jug with thick blue tulip decoration, excellent condition, 15" tall, c. 1868, $495; Burger & Lang, Rochester, N.Y., 2 gal. jug with simple budding flower, excellent condition, 14" tall, c. 1870, $275.

Cortland, N.Y., 1 gal. jug with blue triple flower, 11" tall, c. 1860, $187; Cortland, N.Y., 1 gal. crock with four bud flowers, 5" through line extending from a rim chip on the back, 7-1/2" tall, c. 1870, $176.

Cortland, N.Y., 1 gal. jug with bell flower design, chip at spout and 2 surface chips and a 3" minor hairline at the base in front, 11" tall, c. 1870, $302.50; Unsigned 1/2 gal. jar with lid, slip blue flower decoration, tight freeze line around the base, 7-1/4" tall, c. 1860, $143.

Unsigned 1/2 gal. Cortland jug with pinwheel design, overall staining from use, 9" tall, c. 1870, $302.50; Unsigned 1/2 gal. jar with lid, double bell flower, minor chip in the front and a nickel-size rim chip on the back, 7-1/2" tall, c. 1860, $440.

Cortland, N.Y., 2 gal. crock with multi-flower design, rim chip above the right ear, 9-1/2" tall, c. 1870, $357.50; Cortland, 2 gal. jug with brushed floral design, surface chip at the spout and glued breaks in the handle, 12" tall, c. 1870, $99.

M. Woodruff & Co. Cortland, N.Y., 3 gal. crock with winged eagle decor, professional restoration to tight through lines, 11" tall, c. 1870, $880; Cortland 1 gal. jar with slip decorated flower, large surface chip at the rim in the front, 9" tall, c. 1870, $99.

Brady & Ryan Ellenville, N.Y., 2 gal. crock with thick blue chicken pecking corn, stack mark at the base in the making, 5" tight line on the back and some lime staining, very minor, 9" tall, c. 1885, $577.50.

N. A. White & son, Utica, N.Y., 5 gal. churn, thick blue paddletail design, minor surface chip at the rim, 16-1/2" tall, c. 1885, $1,705; White's, Utica 6 gal. crock with double love birds and "1865" date, professional restoration to rim and base chips, 13-1/2" tall, c. 1865, $2,420.

Unsigned approximate 1 gal. pitcher, slip decorated lines and dots make this decor unique, probably Albany, New York in origin, surface chip at base in the front and a 4" tight line at the rim, 9" tall, c. 1850, $522.50.

Unsigned 6 qt. butter pail with bail handle, tree stump design, "6" in blue script, probably Whites Utica, chips at the spout and 5" through lines extending from the rim, almost 12" tall, c. 1860, $660; White's, 2 gal. jug with running bird, excellent condition, 14" tall, c. 1870, $797.50.

N. A. White & Son, 1 gal. crock with bright blue leaf decor, chip on the ear and interior rim chip, 7" tall, c. 1880, $165; White's Utica 1 gal. jug with vine floral design, 11-1/2" tall, c. 1880, $165.

White's Utica 1 gal. jug with folksy ribbed bird, 11-1/2" tall, c. 1865, $1,045; White's Utica 1 gal. ovoid cream pot with uncommon flower design, very tight lines extending from the rim and a rim chip above the right ear, 8" tall, c. 1865, $302.50.

White's Utica 2 gal. jug with brushed flower design, minor staining from use, 13-1/2" tall, c. 1870, $110; White's Utica 2 gal. jar with a dark blue bird perched on a long petal plume, 7" y-shaped line in back, 11" tall, c. 1865, $440.

T. Harrington, Lyons, N.Y., 6 gal. churn, detailed decoration of a running fox, stabilized j-shaped crack in front extending through the decoration, 19" tall, c. 1855, $5,775.

W.H. Farrah & Co., Geneva, N.Y., 2 gal. preserve jar with 3 glued line cracks, 11" tall, c. 1860, $77; C. Hart & Son, 2 gal. jug with unusual brushed flower, professional restoration to chip at handle & spout, 11" tall, c. 1860, $99.

Geddes, N.Y., 2 gal. crock with simple flower & slip decorated "2" design, rim chip & a short through line on the back, 9" tall, c. 1860, $143; Geddes, N.Y., 2 gal. jug with brushed blue snowflake design, minor surface chip at the spout, 14" tall, c. 1860, $275.

New York Stoneware Co., Ft. Edward, N.Y., 2 gal. crock with chicken pecking corn on ground cover, excellent condition, 9-1/2" tall, c. 1880, $1,210; Ottman Bros. & Co., Ft. Edward, N.Y., 1 gal. crock with tornado design, excellent condition, 7-1/2" tall, c. 1870, $330.

Signed 3 gal. jug with a thick blue bird on a plume, probably Ft. Edward, N.Y., kiln burn & stack mark, 16" tall, c. 1870, $385; Satterlee & Morey, Ft. Edward, 4 gal. jug with thick blue basket of flowers, excellent condition, 17-1/2" tall, c. 1865, $1,760.

Ottman Bros., Ft. Edward, 2 gal. crock with chicken pecking corn, stone ping in the front, otherwise excellent condition, 8" tall, c. 1875, $1,155; Ottman Bros., 2 gal. crock with robin perched on a twig, minor staining from use, 9" tall, c. 1870, $522.50.

Ottman Bros., Ft. Edward, N.Y., 3 gal. crock with large robin perched on a branch, professional restoration to surface chips at the rim, 10-1/2" tall, c. 1870, $467.50; Ottman Bros. & Co., Ft. Edward, 4 gal. crock with large robin perched on a plume, professional restoration to surface chips at the rim, 11-1/2" tall, c. 1870, $385.

E. E. Hall & Co., Boston, 4 gal. crock with a fat bird, full length glued line on the side, lime staining, 11" tall, c. 1880, $247.50; Haxstun & Co., Ft. Edward, 4 gal. crock with leaf design, excellent, 11" tall, c. 1870, $220.

Unsigned 1 gal. crock with thick blue leaf, 5" line from the rim on the back and an interior rim chip, 7-1/2" tall, c. 1860, $99; N.Y., Stoneware Company, 2 gal. jug with floral design, glaze flaking to the front and extensive flaking to the handle and spout, all stable, handle has a large chip where the handle attaches to the base, 14" tall, c. 1870, $55.

Ottman Bros., Ft. Edward, N.Y., 6 gal. cooler with lid, slip blue wreath design, 11" j-shaped glued crack up from the base on the side, 17" tall, c. 1870, $121; New York Stoneware Co., 4 gal. cooler with lid, plume & bird design, excellent condition, 15-1/2" tall, c. 1870, $1,155.

Haxstun Ottman & Co., Ft. Edward, 3 gal. crock with blue floral spray, separation line and stack mark on the back in the making, 10-1/2" tall, c. 1870, $154; Seymour & Bosworth, Hartford, 2 gal. crock with brushed blue dotted bird on plume design, chip at the base, 14" tall, c. 1880, $247.50.

Harrington Burger, 4 gal. pail-shaped crock, thick blue double flower, glued full length crack on the backside & some minor staining, 11-1/4" tall, c. 1853, $770.

John Burger, Rochester, N.Y., 1 gal. pitcher with detailed large flower, 6" long u-shaped glued crack on the backside & 2 other 3" hairlines on the opposite side, surface chip near spout, 11" tall, c. 1865, $797.50.

N. A. White & Son, Utica, N.Y., 3 gal. crock with cobalt flower, excellent condition, c. 1860, $660.

J. & E. Norton, Bennington, V.T., 4 gal. crock with large double flower, bold blue cobalt, professional restoration to long j-shaped line in front through blue and long straight line from rim on very back, 13-1/2" tall, c. 1866, $412.50; J. & E. Norton, Bennington, 3 gal. jug with dotted peacock on stump, professional restoration to the handle, 15" tall, c. 1859, $2,970.

Stoneware Bottles

(This section was prepared by Jim Beedy)

Stoneware was made from clay found principally in New Jersey, Long Island, and upstate New York. Craftsmen who had served a long apprenticeship and worked as journeymen set up small businesses all over the country turning out thousands of pieces of pottery of all kinds. Through the 1840s, much of their product was hand thrown. In the 1850s, molds were more commonly used, saving time, and requiring less skill. They built kilns to fire the raw clay, glazed them inside and out to make them waterproof, and sometimes, decorated them with colored glazes.

Stoneware beer bottles were just one of the many products of the nineteenth century potters. Jugs, crocks, bowls, pitchers, plates and numerous other stoneware products were retailed by the potter or wholesaled to dealers. Beer or soda bottles were sold on order to the bottlers of beverages. The bottler ordered his bottles plain and perhaps painted on or paper labeled his own product. What has made collectors of us is that he frequently ordered his bottles impressed with his name and/or product name and/or place of origin and/or date. Glaze variations, cobalt blue decorations and unusual inscriptions attract us as they also must have attracted the buyers of the product.

Perhaps potters and bottlers started out with the idea of maintaining standard sizes in their bottles, pint (16 oz.), 1/2 pint (8 oz.), and qt. (32 oz.). For reasons not clear to us, they made these sizes plus several in-between sizes. The Ormsby bottle is 8 oz. and the Mariners Pop is 46 oz. Bottles can be found in all sizes in-between, although usually in 1/2 cup (4 oz.)

increments. Potters used templates, the size of the lump of clay they started with and years of experience to quickly turn out these bottles. Contemporary potters believe an early potter could turn out hundreds of bottles in a day. It is not surprising then, that we get some odd ounce capacities.

Nineteenth century bottles were made to be closed with cork stoppers. The large lip was there to hold the string or wire that held the stoppers in against the pressure of carbonation. Later bottles began to have glass bottle stoppers or even lips made for capping with the bottle caps we still use. (See the ginger beers from Rumford, M.E. and Saint John's, Canada.)

Stoneware bottles reigned as beer and soda containers from the 1840s to the 1890s. They had the advantages of being strong (for shipping and reusing), opaque (for protection of the product from light), and retention of temperature (to keep the beer or soda cool in the absence of refrigeration). The major disadvantage was the difficulty in determining the cleanliness for reuse. Perhaps the apocryphal story of someone finding a dead mouse in the bottom of their bottle comes from stoneware days.

Here is a list of some of the beverages contained in stoneware bottles:

Lemon Beer	Sarsaparilla	Omaha Beer
Cream Beer	Pop	Hop Beer
Root Beer	California	Medicated
Mead	Pop	Beer
Spruce	California	
Ale	Pop Beer	

Some of the above such as Mead (fermented honey), Spruce (the fermented tips of Spruce Trees), Ale and Hop Beer we can be pretty sure were alcoholic beverages. Several of the rest probably had an alcohol content, some probably were made for children or teetotalers.

We make root beer to this day that is nonalcoholic. Was 19th century root beer the same? Was cream beer and lemon beer by the same reasoning cream soda and lemonade? Is California Pop and California Pop Beer an alcohol and non alcohol version of the same drink? We still have much to learn about the recipes and brewing processes for these drinks.

When we talk about pricing stoneware beer bottles we are not talking about pricing something like gold where the price is determined in world markets right down to the penny every day. The price is determined when you walk into a shop and see a bottle priced at half what you believe its worth and you can't get it up to the counter fast enough—it makes your day.

The price is also determined when you see a bottle you have been seeking for five years and the price is twice what you thought you should pay, but you have this feeling that you may never see another one so you pay that price. The market doesn't have a manufacturer or wholesaler out there setting a base price that a retailer or buyer can work from. The market for stoneware beers doesn't have a uniformly informed group of retailers selling them. We have attempted here to give "average" or reasonable price ranges for a variety of bottles, knowing that many exceptions can be found. What is certain, is that the value of stoneware beer bottles in general has increased many fold over the last three decades.

Plain unmarked bottles are at the lower end of the scale, and worth $8-$24. Bottles with just a bottler's name or just a product name go for $25-$50. Bottles that have bottler's name and product name, place name or date range from $75-$110. Bottles with some combination of the above plus cobalt blue decoration value at $110-$150. Bottles with the bottler's name or initials hand inscribed in cobalt blue achieve prices from $150-$300.

Other pricing considerations include:

1. A recognition by collectors that some bottles are simply rarer than others.

2. Regional collectors can put a greater demand on bottles from a particular area, driving up prices.

3. An unusual shape or glaze along with more unusual markings may command a higher price. Some of these rarer bottles bring $200-$300.

In the end the price-like beauty is often in the eye of the beholder. If you have questions, comments or interesting bottles I can be reached at: Jim Beedy, P.O. Box 147, Milbridge, ME 04658.

Stoneware Bottles

L. House, unusual shape, made by Louis, Syracuse, N.Y., 1886-1893, 10 oz., $80-$100.

D. L. Ormsby, made by Dorman Leonard, Manhattan, N.Y., 1847-1873, 8 oz., $25-$50.

W. Smith, Greenwich, N.Y., Washington Smith, New York, Potter. The potter's name on the bottle instead of the bottler's is unusual, $250-$300.

J. Jones, Waltham, Mass, "Bottle Not Sold," 1854, $160-$180. The place, name, date, and any other information increases the value of a bottle.

Mariners Pop, bottler unknown, holds 46 oz., one of the largest known stoneware bottles, $110-$130.

Hartleb & Cheltra, Bath, Maine, uncommon bottle from an early bottler from Maine, c. 1840s-1850s, $130-$150.

Smith's White Root bottle, pat. date of July 17, 1866, $100-$120.
Smith and Snow must have sold rights to several other bottlers because Smith's White Root appears with other names like Henry Smith & Hiram Snow of Dover, New Hampshire.

Walls Red Top Root Beer, Springfield, Mass., 1845, Sawtell (on the side), $180-$200.
Sawtell was a Boston bottler and it is unusual to find his name on a Walls bottle from Springfield. The Charles Springfield Brewery dates from about 1845 to 1849.

Pentucket Ale, "Bottle Not Sold," George S. Cushing, Lowell, Mass., 1856, $100-$120.
The bottler considered it very important that his bottles be returned.

Mead, 1902, $70-$90.
The bottle has a mottled glazed top for the honey-based Mead.

Raymond & Fish, unknown bottlers, 10 oz., $25-$50.

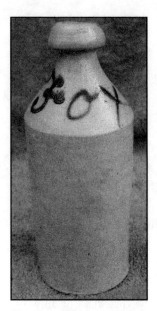

Searings XX, $60-$80. The XX on bottles is open to question. They may have indicated that the contents of the bottle contained alcohol.

Rice & Plummer, 1848, $90-$110. E.W.F. Rice was in Boston from 1848-1851.

Fox, an unknown bottler, $175-$225.

Ginger beer bottles from Maine and Canada that were made in the early 1900s in the "English" style, $150-$200 (each).

J. G. Hall Hop Beer from Joshua, Boston, Mass., 1856, $120-$140.

Moerleins from Cincinnati, Ohio was in business from 1853-1919, $110-$130.

S. C. Zchneil Sour Mash Kiln Dried Grain Whiskey, $130-$150.

C. C. Haley & Co. California Pop, patented October 29, 1872, $110-$130.

This pre-1840 bottle carries no imprint and was made to resemble the classic wine bottle shape, $70-$90.

D. W. Tarr & Co. Cider, from Daniel, Boston, MA., c. 1851-1867, $90-$110.

F. Higgins Ginger Pop, Eastport, ME., c. 1890-1910, $70-$90. The bottle has a "lightning stopper."

B. L. bottle in the shape of a European gin or mineral water bottle though this example is probably American in origin, $80-$100.

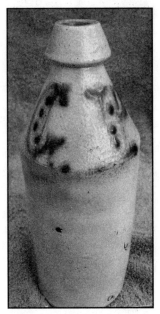

C. P. bottle with decorative cobalt blue from an unknown maker, $250-$300.

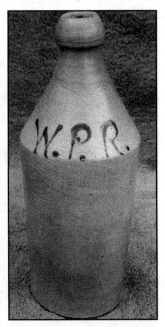

P. Sweeny, Washington Square, Worcester, MA., $100-$130.

J. J. Jerusalem, Chicago, Illinois from Joseph, c. 1868-1887, $60-$80.

W. P. R. lettering in cobalt on this bottle from an unknown maker makes this example especially desirable.

A Collector's Perspective On Buying Stoneware In Today's Market

(Note: This section was prepared by Duane Watson, an avid stoneware collector from the Midwest. The price guide is illustrated with pieces from his personal collection. He is always interested in buying similar pieces and sometimes has pieces to sell. He can be contacted at 1527 Olde Post Road, Ashland, OH 44805 or jwatson@ashland.edu).

I have been earnestly collecting stoneware in virtually all categories since I was 8 years old. I became fascinated with my grandmother's White's Utica 2 gal. fruit jar with a cobalt parrot on a stump design. She used it as an umbrella stand!

Whether New York and New England hand-decorated, Pennsylvania and West Virginia stenciled, Midwestern simple swirls, or blue and white stoneware—I have been on the hunt for it. I hunt in all the typical locations for these treasures of the past: garage sales, flea markets, auctions, mom and pop antique shops, antique malls, and regularly scheduled antique shows. Whenever I can I trek across Ohio, Western New York, Western Pennsylvania, and West Virginia.

During the years, I have seen a dramatic drop in the availability of good quality stoneware. The demand for stoneware is high, and places to hunt for it (attics, cellars, barns) are dwindling. Much stoneware has already been sold into private collections. The demand for stoneware is stemmed, in part, by the country decorating movement that began in the 1970s. A country kitchen is not complete without pieces of stoneware on the counter and in the cupboard. Baby-boomers, myself included, are also collecting for investment or simply a link to the memories of grandpa's farm.

It is extremely rare to find stoneware at garage sales other than the non-decorated, mass-produced molded variety useful for planting flowers or grouping together on a porch for decoration. Flea markets occasionally yield a molded advertising jug or a mini-jug worthy of getting out the checkbook. However, at flea markets you are also likely to find damaged decorated stoneware. Stoneware comes to auction frequently, but usually goes for top or over top dollar. No bargains here, but occasionally a top-end piece of stoneware surfaces that you may be willing to pay the winning bid for.

On the one hand, if you find yourself bidding against dealers, they may have to pull out of the bidding as their profit margin dwindles with the increasing price. As a result, you may buy the piece at a reasonable price. On the other hand, if you have to out-bid another determined collector, you may have to sit on a piece for years before you are able to recover the purchase price. Always remember to keep your perspective.

You can no longer count on mom and pop antique shops to carry stoneware on a regular basis. Owners of such shops tell me that more people are taking their households and collections to auction rather than calling dealers for private sale. Local stoneware collectors bid the pieces too high at auction for dealers to make a profit, so such pieces never see the shop shelves. However, there are those isolated dealers who specialize in stoneware who, even though they are having difficulty finding quantities of stoneware, can be counted on to have a small supply at any time. They may have an army of "pickers" who are looking at all the garage and barn sales in the area in order to sell their finds to the dealer. It also helps to get to know dealers in stoneware and leave your wish list so that when a great piece comes into their shop they can call you.

Larger antique malls usually have a few cases scattered around containing a piece of stoneware or two. It has been my experience that it is often priced at top dollar and beyond, largely to cover the costs of the mall space. In many such malls, if you ask for a discount you can often receive 10%. If you do not ask, you often will not receive! Some malls will go further and allow you to offer a counter-bid that the front desk will call into the dealer while you shop. Occasionally a bird in the hand is worth two in the bush and the dealer will accept your offer. However, do not expect to ultimately receive more than a 20% to 25% discount.

Larger antique shows offer a variety of stoneware because it is the gathering place of all those who have attended the sales, auctions, and malls. It is often where newly acquired pieces are brought first. There is often quite a disparity at shows between the quality and prices of similar pieces, so treasures at bargain prices can be found as well as over-priced junk. Later in the show day, as the crowds thin out, dealers are often more willing to bargain. However, if you were waiting until the end of a show to make an offer for a top-end piece, it will likely be already

boxed and on its way to someone else's collection.

For those of you who are connected to the Internet, the ebay on-line antique auction house and other such auctions have a stoneware category. Each piece is usually carefully described and accompanied by a picture or two. Stoneware is usually auctioned for one week. After you register as a buyer-seller you can bid on any piece that interests you.

This new format is bound to change the way people collect stoneware. A quick surf of the offerings on the net shows that there are marginal pieces as well as museum pieces offered, and everything in between. The truly good pieces are bringing market prices and beyond. Often there are no bargains here, because knowledgeable and motivated buyers are vying with one another for the same pieces. However, very good pieces can be purchased at market price. Since each piece has to be described so carefully, I suspect that people will be more careful in initially purchasing stoneware knowing that each imperfection will have to be described if they plan to resell it on the Internet.

Despite the current high demand for stoneware, the lower-end pieces of molded and advertising stoneware (the Midwestern crocks with the bullseyes and bees) are still available and affordable. The more expensive stoneware from the Northeast and elaborately stenciled and freehand stoneware from West Virginia and Western Pennsylvania sell to a smaller group of stoneware collectors willing to sacrifice large sums to fill gaps in their collections. It moves fast, so if you are planning to attend an antique show, be there when the show opens.

There are always surprises that keep stoneware collecting interesting. Older collectors are continually disbanding collections and placing better pieces on the market. Just when you have endured months of empty searching, you spot a Bennington jug with a bird that has been on a collector's shelf for 35 years waiting to go home with you (for a small fortune). Or you are at a flea market and someone decided that it was time for grandma to empty out the barn and they rented a table for a day and there is that West Virginia canning jar stenciled with that obscure town name that you have always wanted (for next to nothing)!

This demand for high-end pieces has spurred a growth industry in repairs. Missing handles are being restored, cracks painted and glazed over, and even crazing drawn in with pencil. It really does not matter whether a dealer is honest or not these days. Repair work is often so good, that even honest dealers can be burned by a repair and be totally unaware of it until you point it out. This makes buying from local dealers with reputations to maintain, or dealers who specialize in stoneware the safer bet. An honest local dealer will probably refund your money if you find a repair in a reasonable time after purchase.

Often a stoneware dealer will be able to spot repairs before you purchase the piece. In any case, before you buy, you need to carefully examine every piece of better stoneware for repair work. Your personal preferences come into play here. I do not mind a minor lip chip being repaired, but I want nothing to do with a handle replacement unless the design is extremely unusual on the piece (e.g., tiger, deer.)

Stay knowledgeable about stoneware in general and current prices. Read books about stoneware and its manufacture. Learn about local potters whose pottery may be in high demand in your area and can still be found. As you search for stoneware, continue to compare prices on similar pieces and eventually you will have a good idea when something is under or over the average asking price. Do not make auction prices as the standard, for they are often the price only one or two determined individuals are willing to pay for a piece. One guide I always use is to ask myself if I tried to sell the piece I am about to buy, would it be reasonable to expect anyone else to pay that price from me.

The following price guide features pieces that I have found during my hunting expeditions. They are presented in three successive groupings: New England-New York, Pennsylvania-West Virginia, and the Midwest. I am particularly thankful to Karen and Ed Bertsch, formerly of Norton, Ohio, who recently sold me the pick of their stoneware collection when they semi-retired from the antique business. Many of the better pieces featured here once graced their fine collection. I also want to thank my friends and fellow avid collectors, Phil and Barb Hostetler of Dalton, Ohio, who gave me the benefit of their knowledge for my price guide.

Stoneware Price Guide

C. Crolius, Manhattan-Wells, NY, 3-gal. jug with shoulder swag, $700-$900.

I. Seymour, Troy, NY, 2 gal. jug with cobalt flower, $350-$450.

Early Midwestern 2 gal. ovoid jug with cobalt flower, probably NE Ohio, $275-$350.

White's Utica, NY, 2 gal. jug with stylized flower bouquet, $350-$450.

John Burger, Rochester, NY, 3 gal. jug with elaborate cobalt flower, $600-$800.

A. O. Whittemore, Havana, NY, 3 gal. jug with compote of flowers, rare design, $900-$1,200.

Cowden and Wilcox, Harrisburg, PA, 1 gal. jug with cobalt flower, $375-$425.

From left: S. T. Brewer, Havana, NY, 2 gal. jug with brushed double cobalt flower, $300-$350; F. B. Norton and Co., Worcester, Mass., 2-gal. jug with brushed cobalt plume, $300-$350.

Evan Jones, Pittston, PA, 3 gal. crock with typical Jones horizontal brushed cobalt tulip, $300-$400.

From left: White's, Utica, NY, 1 gal. jug with White's typical cobalt slip Christmas tree and oak leaf designs, $175-$225 each.

From left: Lyons Stoneware Co., Lyons, NY, Merchant's jug, 2 gal., "Henry Dautermann, 1224-26, Fillmore Ave., Buffalo, NY," $200-$250; Merchant's jug, 1-gal., "C. N. Guerliu, 334 Warren St., Hudson, N.Y.," $175-$225.

Merchant's jug, 3 gal., "Jones, Dealer in Dry Goods, Groceries, Paint, Hard Ware, Pulaski, NY," attributed to S. Hart, Oswego, NY, $400-$500.

Merchant's jug, 1 gal., "Battles and Millard, Liquor Dealers, Albion, NY," $350-$450.

White's, Utica, NY, 1 gal. preserve jar with cobalt parrot on a stump, $500-$600.

Unsigned 3 gal. chicken pecking corn crock with lid, $800-$1,200.

M. W. Woodruff, Cortland, NY, 3 gal. cream pot with double tulip design, $350-$450.

Kenner, Davidson, and Miller, Strasburg, VA, 1 gal. jar with freehand decoration, $400-$500.

Merchant's canner, 1 gal., "Roth and Wendel, Staple and Fancy Groceries, 3801 Jacob St., Wheeling, W.VA.," $300-$350.

From left: White's, Utica, NY, 2 gal. preserve jar with White's typical orchid design, $275-$325; Lyons, NY, 2 gal. preserve jar with oak leaf, $225-$275.

From left: E. and L. P. Norton, Bennington, VT, 1 gal. crock with Norton's typical cobalt leaf design, $225-$250; S. Hart, Oswego, NY, 1 gal. crock with brushed cobalt flower, $225-$250; unsigned 1-gal. crock with vivid cobalt slip flower, with cover, $175-$225.

Evan Jones, Pittston, PA, 3 gal. crock with typical Jones horizontal brushed cobalt tulip, $300-$400.

Unsigned 1-1/2 qt. preserve jars with floral swags, $175-$225 each.

Unsigned, 1-1/2 qt. canner with stripes and freehand vine design, western Pennsylvania, $400-$500.

Early Pennsylvania 2 gal. jar with cobalt tulips, $350-$450.

White's, Utica, NY, 5 gal. churn with elaborate cobalt slip orchid design, $2,000-$2,500.

White's, Utica, NY, 3 gal. churn with elaborate cobalt slip orchid design, $1,500-$2,000.

Merchant's jar, 1 gal., "Alderman and Scott, Belpre, Ohio" with rare stenciled birds and bees design, $600-$800.

Star Pottery, 1 qt. canner, Greensboro, PA, with stenciled eagle, rare, $900-$1,200.

Eagle Pottery, 3 qt. canner with stenciled eagle, rare, $1,200-$1,500.

From left: Unsigned 1 qt. canner with cobalt florishes and cover, $145-$165; P. Hermann, Baltimore, Maryland, 1 gal. jar with double flower on each side, $225-$250; unsigned 1-1/2 qt. canner, with a band of flowers around the middle, $165-$185.

H. Cowden, Harrisburg, PA, 4 gal. crock with brushed cobalt triple flower design, $300-$400.

From left: 2 unsigned, 1-1/2 qt. canners with 4 cobalt stripes, $175-$195; unsigned 1 qt. canner with 5 stripes, $175-$200.

From left: unsigned, 1 qt. canner with stenciled rose design attributed to Hamilton and Jones, Greensboro, PA, $200-$250; 1-1/2 qt. canner with stenciled bouquet of flowers, $275-$325.

Hamilton and Jones, Greensboro, PA, 2 gal. jar with stencil and freehand vine work, $750-$1,000.

James Hamilton and Co., Greensboro, PA, 2 gal. cream pot with stenciled rose design, $400-$500.

Williams and Reppert, Greensboro, PA, 2 gal. jug with stencil and freehand, $300-$400.

Unsigned early ovoid 3 gal. crock, with floral garland around both sides, $500-$700.

J. Weaver, 6 gal. ovoid crock with elaborate garland on the front, $800-$900.

Unsigned, 3 gal. jar with stencil and freehand work, $400-$500.

Jas. Hamilton and Co., Greensboro, PA, 3 gal. jar with elaborate bell flower stenciled design, $400-$500.

From left: Hamilton and Jones, or James Hamilton, Greensboro, PA 1-1/2 qt. canners with lily pad, leaf, and rising sun stenciled designs, $195-$225 each.

Flack and Van Arsdale, Cornwall, Ontario, 2 gal. crock with cobalt slip bird on a branch, $500-$700.

From left: Hamilton and Jones, Greensboro, PA, 1 gal. jars with 8 stripes and stencil, $275-$325 and stenciled rose, $350-$400.

A. Conrad, New Geneva, PA, 2 gal. jars with stenciled rose and rosebud designs, $275-$325 each.

T. F. Reppert, "Successor to Jas. Hamilton and Co., Greensboro, PA"; 4 gal. storage jar with stencil and freehand, $400-$500.

Williams and Reppert, Greensboro, PA, 4 gal. storage jar with stencil and freehand design, $400-$500.

Hamilton and Jones, Greensboro, PA, 5 gal. storage jar with elaborate stencil and freehand vine work, rare, $1,800-$2,200.

Jas. Hamilton and Co., Greensboro, PA, 8 gal. storage jar with stencil and freehand design, $900-$1,200.

A. P. Donaghho, Parkersburg, W.VA, 8 gal. storage jar with cover, $400-$700.

A. P. Donaghho, Parkersburg, W. VA., 4 gal. storage with stenciled zipper design, $300-$400.

Unsigned milk pitcher with floral garland, $600-$750.

From left: Hamilton and Jones, Greensboro, PA, 2 gal. preserve jar with cobalt freehand and stencil design, $300-$350; Williams and Reppert, Greensboro, PA, 2 gal. preserve jar with cobalt freehand and stencil design, $300-$350.

T. F. Reppert, Greensboro, PA, butter crock with the advertising, "Manufacturer Best Blue Stoneware," $400-$500.

From left: Hamilton and Jones, Greensboro, PA, 1-1/2 gal. apple butter crock with stenciled bird with a branch in its mouth, $350-$450; Hamilton and Jones Manufacturers, Greensboro, PA, 1 gal. apple butter crock with elaborate stencil, $250-$300.

Midwestern "Bee" crocks, $95-$125 each.

Unsigned 1-1/2 qt. churn with original dasher, $200-$250.

Midwestern, 3 gal. jug with freehand flower, $225-$275.

Ohio, 6-gal. ovoid crock, with elaborate flower, $400-$600.

Midwestern, 5 gal. crock with elaborate brushed cobalt flower, $250-$300.

Midwestern, 3 gal. churn with deep cobalt flower, $400-$500.

Midwestern, 6 gal. crock with elaborate tornado design and cover, $225-$250.

Midwestern, 4 gal. churn with stenciled eagle and banner reading "E Pluribus Unum," $400-$500.

Unsigned freehand decorated butter crocks, $225-$250 for the smaller; $250-$275 for the larger.

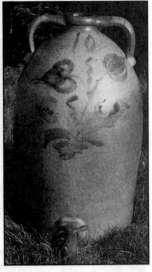

J. Fisher, Lyons, NY, 3 gal. crock with dragonfly design, $150-$200.

White and Wood, Binghampton, NY, 4 gal. cream pot with deep cobalt bird on a branch design, $600-$800.

Midwestern, 10 gal. water cooler with double handles and elaborate bouquet of brushed cobalt flowers, $700-$900.

Unsigned milk pans with freehand three leaf clover designs, $350-$450 for the smaller; $450-$550 for the larger.

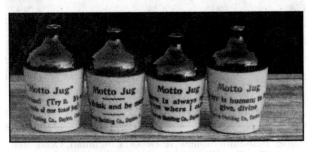

Motto mini-jugs from the Detrick Distilling Co., Dayton, Ohio, $85-$110 each.

Midwestern, 6 gal. crock with elaborate brushed cobalt flowers in a compote, $275-$325.

Midwestern, 4 gal. crock with elaborate flower, $250-$300.

Red Wing Stoneware, Red Wing, MN, 10 gal. crock with butterfly/flower combination, unsigned, $300-$400.

Midwestern, 6 gal. crock with elaborate tornado design and cover, $225-$250.

Midwestern, 4 gal. water cooler with freehand flower, $350-$450.

Unsigned milk bowl with freehand tulip design, $300-$350.

Unsigned spittoon with freehand tulips, rare, $500-$750.

James Benjamin Stoneware Depot, Cincinnati, Ohio, stenciled pieces, $145-$175 for the jug, $175-$195 for the canner with cover.

242

Stile's jugs from Cleveland, Ohio, patented 1892, $125-$145 for the advertising jugs; $95-$110 for the molasses jugs.

Field hand's jug, Dustman Pottery, Berlin Center, Ohio, $125-$150.

From left: White's Utica covered butter with stag hunting scene, $400-$500; White's Utica canteen advertising Bardwell's Root Beer, $600-$800.

Robinson Clay Products covered butters from Akron, Ohio, largest to smallest: $350-$400; $325-$350; $275-$300; $225-$250.

CHAPTER 7

$\mathcal{T}$HE TEST

Final Examination #16

This is the sixteenth examination that we have prepared in this series. Most have been met with critical dispassion or disdain. A reviewer from a junior high newspaper in Idaho found it, "generally sophomoric in tone, but at the same time, juvenile in presentation." He went on to add, "I picked it up and couldn't put it down." We later learned that the ink on several of the pages in his review copy was at the crux of his dilemma.

Directions: Read each question carefully. Minimal effort has been made not to confuse and disorient you. Select the single best response to each question, reflect upon it, and feel free to second guess yourself.

1. **This chair dates from**
   a. after 1850 but before 1900
   b. after 1900 but before 1940
   c. it appears to be a reproduction

2. **It could have originally been used in**
   a. a fire station
   b. a country store
   c. a land fill
   d. a & b
   e. none of the above

3. **Chairs of this form have been described as "_____" Windsors.**

4. **The chair is worth about**
   a. $40
   b. $100
   c. $200
   d. $400

5. This piece of fishing gear is called a
   _____.

6. True or False
An item like this should be worth at least $40.

7. True or False
This cupboard dates from about 1820.

8. What color would add the most to the value of the cupboard?
a. red
b. green
c. brown
d. blue
e. all are equally valuable

9. True or False
This cupboard could be described as a step-back.

10. True or False
The cupboard is also a "blind front" with 16 "lights."

11. True or False
This cupboard is worth a least $1,500.

12. True or False
This chair is a classic Boston rocker.

13. True or False
The chair dates prior to 1870.

---

14. Antique Week is held each August in
a. Colorado
b. New York
c. Pennsylvania
d. New Hampshire

15. The *Bee* is published in
a. Pennsylvania
b. New York

c. Ohio
d. none of the above

16. *M.A.D.* is published in
a. Mississippi
b. Missouri
c. Maine
d. Memphis

17. True or False, This spice chest could have been sold at Sears-Roebuck in 1915.

18. It appears to be worth about
a. $50
b. $150
c. $300
d. more than $400

19. If this chest was painted white, the value would
a. be depleted
b. rise
c. go down
d. a & c

20. The apricot label
  a. enhances the value of the firkin
  b. would be worth at least another
    $100 if it said "Shaker"
  c. both a & b are correct

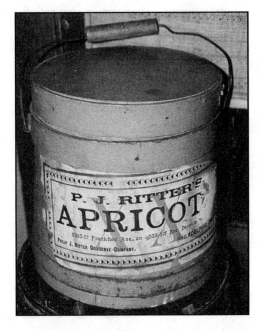

21. Most butter prints are made of
  a. walnut
  b. pine
  c. poplar
  d. maple

22. True or False
The "bird" butter stamp or print is worth at least $205.

23. True or False
It is a little known fact that more red-ware was made in Wisconsin than in Pennsylvania.

24. True or False
Redware is fired at a higher tempera-ture than stoneware and that is what gives it the red color.

25. True or False

This box was factory-made about 1910.

26. True or False

The box is probably made of walnut or maple.

27. **Which of the states below contained Shaker communities at one point in their history?**

__Illinois   __New York
__Ohio   __Kentucky
__Wisconsin   __California
__South Dakota   __Iowa

28. **The watch repair & diamonds sign is worth**
   a. $100-$200
   b. $300-$500
   c. $600-$1,000
   d. $1,200-$2,000

29. A quick glance at this jug should tell you

__it was made in New York State
__it is Midwestern in origin
__it has been "thrown"
__worth more than $100
__worth more than $1,000

---

30. True or False

This is an example of a "thrown" canning jar.

31. True or False

If this jar was covered with Albany slip, it could have been produced at the Peoria (IL) Pottery.

32. The "heart in hand"
__was part of a Masonic Lodge
__was used in an IOOF initiation
__is worth more than $750
__dates from about 1820
__is made of molded resin

33. The seat in this chair is made of
a. cherry
b. oak
c. poplar
d. pine

34. True or False

These cast iron horses' heads are probably reproduction.

35. True or False

The sleeping cat is made of chalk and dates from about 1830.

36. True or False

The cat is made of plaster-of-Paris and dates after 1900.

37. The sleeping cat is worth about
   a. $25-$40
   b. $65-$75
   c. more than $150

38. If the station was owned by Mork and Mindy, the value would be
   a. enhanced
   b. diminished
   c. doesn't make any difference

39. Which of the gentlemen below should have worked at Mork's?
   a. Montgomery Clift
   b. Bud Abbott
   c. Sal Mineo
   d. Robin Williams

40. True or False

This kettle is probably not
__dovetailed
__English in origin
__worth more than $150
__going to be in huge demand at the
 show on the corner next weekend

41. True or False

The kettle could be earlier and more
valuable if it was made of cast iron.

42. This pitcher

__is "hand thrown"
__can be described as sponge
 decorated
__dates from before 1850
__is probably lined with Albany slip
__is probably not "marked"

43. True or False

This pitcher is worth a minimum of
$135.

44. Check the description that accurately represents the collection of woodenware

___probably made from cherry or pine

___factory-made

45. True or False

This Schoenhut clown was made after 1940.

See page 254 for the answers.

Scoring Scale

46-50 points: You and a guest are eligible for a week at your expense at Vivian's Collectibles & Crafts Mall in Buffalo, NY. The trip must be taken in January or February and includes all seminars, special dealer nights, dough-nut tasting sessions, and walking tours of the facility.

40-45 points: You and two guests are eligible for two weeks at your expense at Vivian's in Buffalo. This trip must be taken in January. Note: Please bring an extra coat because the heat at the mall is not dependable.

35-39 points: You and a guest will get to spend two days with the winners for a debriefing session upon their return from Buffalo.

Less than 35 points: An auto-graphed 4" x 5" picture of Vivian who will be depicted repiling her booth. Please do not request personalizations or inscriptions. Since the accident she does not write well.

Answers to Quiz #16

1. b
2. d
3. firehouse
4. b
5. creel
6. true
7. false-later
8. d
9. true
10. false
11. true
12. false-It's a Salem rocking chair.
13. true
14. d
15. d (Conn.)
16. c
17. true
18. b
19. d
20 .c
21. d
22. true
23. false
24. false
25. false
26. false-pine
27. Ohio, New York, Kentucky

28. b
29 Midwestern, molded
30. false
31. true
32. IOOF initiation; worth more than $750
33. d
34. true
35. false-much later
36. true
37. b
38. a, b, or c-This is a gift that you probably need at this point.
39. d
40. dovetailed; English in origin; worth more than $150; if all the beanies and Longaberger baskets are gone, it may sell.
41. true
42. sponge decorated; not marked
43. true
44. factory-made
45. false-The company closed in the 1930s.